Canada A Portrait

THE OFFICIAL HANDBOOK OF PRESENT CONDITIONS AND RECENT PROGRESS • 54TH EDITION PUBLISHED UNDER THE AUTHORITY OF THE MINISTER OF INDUSTRY, SCIENCE AND TECHNOLOGY

The National Library of Canada has catalogued
this publication as follows:

Main entry under title:

Canada : a portrait

54th ed.
Biennial
''The official handbook of present conditions and recent progress.''
Issued also in French under title: Un Portrait du Canada, ISSN 0840-6022.
Continues: Canada handbook, the. . . handbook of present
conditions and recent progress.
ISBN 0-660-14558-8
ISSN 0840-6014
DSS Cat. no. CS11-403E

1. Canada – Economic conditions – Periodicals.
2. Canada – Social conditions – Periodicals.
3. Canada – Politics and government – Periodicals.
4. Canada – Description and travel – Periodicals.
5. Canada – Handbooks, manuals, etc. I. Statistics Canada.
Communications Division.

D.W. Friesen & Sons Ltd.
Altona, Manitoba

FC51.C35   971   C89-079097-3
F1008.C35

FOREWORD *Canada: A Portrait* is a unique and innovative part of Statistics Canada's publishing program. Combining colour photographs of Canada with information on the social, cultural and economic life of the country, it presents a rich and lively look at the major trends and challenges facing the country.

This 54th edition of *Canada: A Portrait* continues the tradition of providing substantial and clear reportage on all sectors of the country – the land, the people, the society, the arts and the economy.

This year, I am pleased to introduce a new and expanded format with many innovations. I am especially honoured to introduce the contributions of six eminent Canadians who have presented us with their "portraits" or perceptions of Canada. Many thanks to Roberta Bondar, Jean Béliveau, Douglas Cardinal, Tomson Highway, Antonine Maillet and W.O. Mitchell.

Other new features include a first-ever chapter on Canada's place within the world community, called "Canada in the World" and a full colour "art gallery" which showcases Canadian contemporary art and helps us, therefore, to draw an even larger picture or "portrait" of Canada.

Indeed, the sustaining strength of *Canada: A Portrait* has always been its commitment to presenting Canada to Canadians through the eyes of other Canadians. Since 1992 was the commemorative year of Canada's Confederation, it seems particularly apt to introduce as many of these perspectives as possible.

As an enduring and informative record of our land and our people, this edition of *Canada: A Portrait* should offer much to the understanding of this great and dynamic country.

Ivan P. Fellegi

Chief Statistician of Canada

ACKNOWLEDGEMENTS The 1993 edition of *Canada: A Portrait* reflects the commitment and creativity of many people. On behalf of Statistics Canada, it is my great pleasure to acknowledge and thank these people and to note the excellence and innovation of their endeavours.

Special thanks and acknowledgement to Jim Reil, who headed the editorial team for *Canada: A Portrait*. On the team were David Blais, Alan Sharpe, Keane Shore and Lauren Walker. Denis Bernard headed the French editorial component, with help from Chantal Prévost and Martin Blais. Pat Harris helped prepare all charts and graphs. In addition, Marg Smith, senior editor for the team, provided very valued guidance and sharp insights, bringing her many years of experience to bear on the completion of this project.

Special thanks to David Blais, production manager, and Linda MacDonald, production assistant, for their excellent work. Invaluable help was provided by Systems and Production, headed by Diane Leblanc, who was assisted by colleagues Elaine Brassard, Natacha Cousineau, Chantal Caron and Colette O'Meara.

Canada: A Portrait was reviewed by referees within Statistics Canada. Their astute guidance and insights are greatly appreciated. Many thanks to Philip Cross, Jean Dumas, Ken Korporal, Iain McKellar, Craig McKie and Stewart Wells.

Special thanks also to Jim Power and John MacCraken for co-ordinating the design team, which included Mike McAuliffe, Renée Saumure, Cheryl Vincent and Roberto Guido, and to Johanne Beauseigle for managing the complex challenge of typesetting. Superb technical support was provided by Marc Pelchat, Pierre Groulx, Benoît Fontaine and Guy Berthiaume. Much appreciation to Diane Joanisse, who headed composition with support from Rachel Mondou, Suzanne Beauchamp, Sue Lineger, Ginette Meilleur, Jean-Marie Lacombe, Rose-Marie Andrews and Ann Trépanier. Special thanks also to Barbara Elliott and Jacques Tessier, who managed printing liaison. Many thanks also to Katherine Bonner and Suzanne Joberty for superb marketing initiatives and to Alain Mazet of Secretary of State for translation services.

Statistics Canada wishes to especially acknowledge the work of Neville Smith and Aviva Furman in the redesign of *Canada: A Portrait*. Their energetic and evocative designs have supported and enhanced the editorial content of this book. Also, a very special thanks to Frank Mayrs for photo research and selection, and to Daniel Sharp for his thoughtful selection of the contemporary Canadian art gallery.

Appreciation and thanks are extended to all contributors from government departments and agencies who throughout the years have provided invaluable information to Statistics Canada in the development of this publication.

*C*anada: A Portrait is prepared under the aegis of the Communications Division, headed by Director Wayne Smith, with the collaboration and support of the Publications Division, under Assistant Director David Roy. It has been my privilege to be mentored and guided by these people in the management of this project.

Jonina Wood

Editor-in-Chief, *Canada: A Portrait*

OUR THANKS TO YOU... Statistics Canada wishes to thank the millions of Canadians who respond to our surveys and who make it possible for us to provide the kind of up-to-date information so necessary to the well-being of Canada.

Without this important partnership, publications like *Canada: A Portrait* would not be possible.

From all of us at Statistics Canada, our many thanks.

TABLE OF CONTENTS

4   This Land
4   Canada's Natural Regions
10   The Human Landscape
21   Canada's Climate
27   Environmental Issues

34   The People
34   The Immigrant Experience
37   The Changing Canadian Family
39   Marriage and Divorce
39   Growing Older
41   Canada: Many Peoples, Many Languages
43   Religion
45   The First Nations: Canada's Aboriginal Peoples
47   Provincial and Territorial Snapshots

58   The Society
58   The Government and Legal System
67   Communications
73   Education
76   Health and Social Security

84   Arts and Leisure
85   At Centre Stage: Canada's Performing Arts
90   Preserving the Past: Canada's Heritage
92   Literature and Publishing
97   Going to the Movies
101   Broadcasting

105   Using Our Leisure Time

110   Visions of Canada
110   Images of Contemporary Canadian Art

134   The Economy
134   Canada's Key Economic Players
142   An Economic Overview
147   Canada's Diverse Economic Landscape
151   Our Economic Life

160   Canada in the World
160   Canada's Economic Impact
166   Canada Snapshots
171   Canada in the World Community

177   Photographic Credits

182   Bibliography/Selected Sources

187   Statistics Canada Regional Reference Centres

192   Index

199   Map of Canada's Natural Regions

201   Map of Canada

The elders tell us that we must learn to love the mountain streams, and the wind on our brows, and that the roots of our feet must reach into the ground. We and the earth are one – what we do to the land we do to one another. Canada is a unique land of dramatic seasons, colours and textures, from the Rockies to the Prairies to the eastern seacoast. The drama of this land requires that we connect with it, harmonize with it, honour it.

As an architect, I rely on the forms of nature for the shapes of my buildings. As a Canadian, I am happy to contribute my vision. If we all contribute our visions, in our own ways, honouring each person's uniqueness, then together we will build a nation of which our elders are proud.

Douglas Cardinal, born in Calgary, Alberta. Architect, designer of the Canadian Museum of Civilization.

$\mathcal{T}$HIS $\mathcal{L}$AND

Canada's geography challenges the imagination. Imagine a country where Newfoundlanders live closer to Africans in Gambia than they do to fellow Canadians in British Columbia. Or a country with an island (Ellesmere Island) that has a glacier bigger than Ireland. Imagine a country with two million lakes, and the world's longest coastline – but that shares a border with only one nation, the United States.

This is Canada, so vast that it spans six time zones and fronts three oceans – Atlantic, Pacific and Arctic. With a land area of nearly 10 million square kilometres, Canada is the largest country in the Western Hemisphere, stretching over half of the North American continent and totalling nearly 7% of the earth's surface.

Canada's southernmost point, Middle Island in Lake Erie, shares the same latitude as the French Riviera and Rome. The country's northernmost point, Cape Columbia on Ellesmere Island, is only 768 kilometres from the North Pole. Between these two points are more than 4 600 kilometres of mostly wilderness, wildlife and silence.

Even greater than this north-south span is Canada's breadth. About 5 500 kilometres – one-quarter of the distance around the world – separate Cape Spear in Newfoundland from the Yukon-Alaska border.

Canada's physical diversity is just as spectacular: towering mountain ranges and fertile lowlands; immense areas of boreal forest and frigid northern tundra; vast plains and innumerable scattered lakes.

And yet Canada's landforms, along with its harsh climate, have confined development. About 89% of the country has never been permanently settled. Only Prince Edward Island – Canada's smallest province – is completely inhabited. "Canada," as former prime minister Pierre Elliott Trudeau pointed out, "is not a country for the cold of heart or the cold of feet."

In this chapter, discover a large-canvas portrait of Canada, from the Arctic to the Pacific to the Atlantic: a panorama of this land's remarkable natural regions, its diverse human landscape, and its challenging climate.

Canada's Natural Regions

Canada comprises several distinct natural regions. These are the Arctic Archipelago, the Western Cordillera, the Great Plains, the Precambrian Shield, the Great Lakes-St. Lawrence Lowlands, and the Appalachians. These regions took shape during the last 4.5 billion years as the earth's continents separated and drifted together again in new places. Rocks formed from ocean sediments were buckled into mountain ranges or were thrust up along joints and faults. Once above the level of the oceans, these ranges were battered by wind, sea and rain.

Then the Ice Age came. A million years ago, during the Pleistocene epoch, the world was much colder than it is today, and massive glaciers covered much of Canada, Northern Europe and the mountainous areas of Asia. At the peak of the Pleistocene, 97% of Canada was buried in ice up to 3 kilometres thick. This ice sheet disappeared more than 10,000 years ago, but it left its mark on the land. As the glaciers receded north, they exerted tremendous pressures on the earth, scouring out hollows and valleys that soon filled with water. They stripped soil, minerals and rocks, later depositing this material in valleys and plains when the ice melted. Most Canadians live on these glacial deposits, and glaciers still cover 2% of the country. During this period, humans – unable to cope with the harsh climate in the north – remained in tropical and sub-tropical regions further south.

Arctic Tundra and Islands   Surrounding Hudson Bay, and extending north of the tree line to the edge of the Arctic Ocean, lies the tundra – a vast plain carpeted with mosses, lichens, dwarf shrubs and grasses. Here the summer heat rarely melts the ice in the ground, and so it remains permanently frozen, making development difficult and farming impossible. This permafrost covers 40% of Canada, and in the Arctic reaches depths of almost half a kilometre.

Almost 900 species of flowering plants sprout from the tundra each summer. Although annual precipitation is low, the permafrost prevents drainage and leaves the mossy undergrowth sodden; the midnight sun from June until August does the rest. Some plants – such as the arctic poppy – flower and go to seed in less than a month.

Our Wandering North Magnetic Pole The earth's north magnetic pole is Canadian – for the moment. In one hundred years it may be on the Russian Federation's side of the Arctic Ocean.

Today it's located amongst the Queen Elizabeth Islands, some 1 400 kilometres south of the north geographic pole. But it's on the move. Every 24 hours, the north magnetic pole completes a clockwise ellipse centred on its mean position. During magnetically active days, it wanders up to 80 kilometres from its average position. This mean position is also drifting northward.

The earth's north magnetic pole was discovered by Sir James Clark Ross, the British polar explorer. He found it at Cape Adelaide in 1831, 900 kilometres south of its current position. Although the cairn that Ross built no longer marks the spot, his discovery enabled scientists to better understand the shape of the earth's magnetic field, and thus to produce better magnetic charts for today's Arctic explorers and navigators.

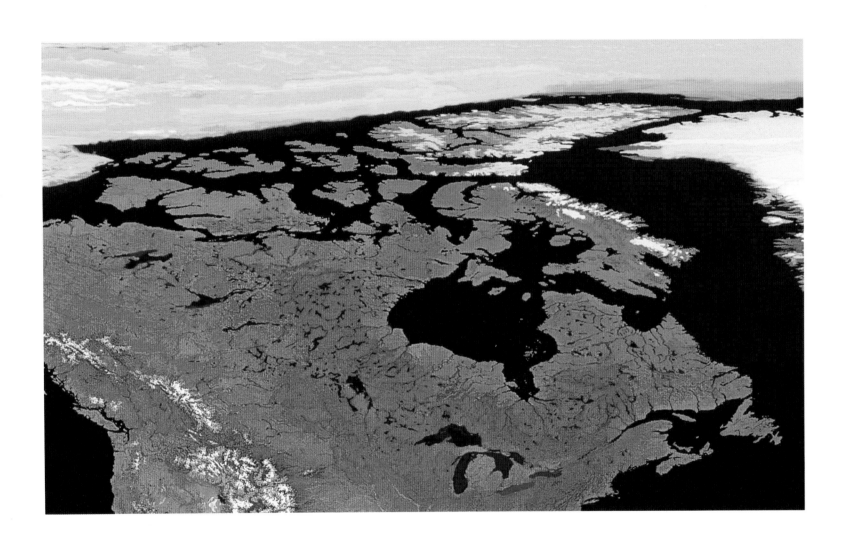

VIEW OF CANADA FROM SPACE.
(OPPOSITE PAGE)

The tundra also supports a tremendous variety of wildlife. Between 300,000 and 500,000 caribou graze the summer feeding grounds. Musk oxen roam the valley meadows; thousands of beluga whales calve in the warm shallows of Cunningham Inlet on Somerset Island. Polar bears, ringed seals, walruses and killer whales inhabit the coasts.

North of the tundra are the hundreds of islands of the Arctic Ocean. Shaped like a great triangle, this archipelago spans 2 800 kilometres from east to west, and stretches 1 800 kilometres to the northern tip of Canada. Four of the islands are enormous; Baffin Island alone is nearly twice the size of New Zealand. The Arctic Ocean has full ice cover throughout the year, but ocean currents shift the ice flows about. Navigating large ships through the openings – as the North West Passage explorers first did – is dangerous work even today.

Western Cordillera Forced up by buckling continental plates some 60 million years ago, then sculpted by glaciers and partially drowned by the sea, the colossal Cordillera range of mountains dominates the western quarter of the country (British Columbia and Alberta). A vast rocky spine running south to north – more than 2 400 kilometres long and about 725 kilometres wide – Canada's Western Cordillera stretches from the 49th parallel to the Arctic Ocean.

The Cordillera comprises a western mountain range bordering the Pacific Ocean, an eastern system facing the Great Plains, and plateaus and lesser ranges in between.

The steep coastal mountains shelve into the sea, their magnificence enhanced by deep fjords indenting the coastline. Because few gaps through this formidable range are suitable for travel, the Fraser River Valley and the gap at Prince Rupert, British Columbia, are tremendously important. It is through these locations that the trans-Canada road and rail systems pass.

Northwards, the coastal range runs into the St. Elias Mountains in northwestern British Columbia and adjacent Yukon and Alaska. Here reign Canada's high and mighty – the tallest mountains in the country. Mount Logan in the Yukon at 5 951 metres is Canada's highest, and 16 of its noble family in the Yukon alone command heights of more than 4 000 metres.

Amidst these giants lie small areas of lowlands, mostly in the lower Fraser River Valley and in southeastern Vancouver Island. The irrigated fertile valleys in the south include the Okanagan, well known for its vineyards and fruit and vegetable farms.

East of the Cordillera lie the Rocky Mountains, with at least 55 peaks over 3 000 metres. Although their rocks were formed from ocean deposits 500 million years ago, the actual mountains were folded, faulted and overthrust by the earth's forces about 400 million years later.

Great Plains The Great Plains are a seemingly endless expanse of what Albertan author W. O. Mitchell called "the least common denominator of nature . . . land and sky." Glaciers bulldozed this region flat during the last Ice Age, depositing in the south, topsoil, clay and minerals scraped from the Canadian Shield and

seven

nearby mountains. A vast area of water-retentive soils – ideal for growing wheat and general farming – was the result.

The dry southwest – the southernmost part of Alberta and Saskatchewan – is a semi-arid land of short grass. To the north is the wheat-growing crescent, with its fertile soil and higher rainfall, where wild grasses once grew shoulder high. Scattered throughout the grasslands are more than 8 million sloughs (small ponds) and potholes, the breeding grounds for half of North America's ducks, geese, swans and pelicans.

North of the wheat belt is rolling aspen parkland, the transition zone between the prairie and the boreal (northern) forest and tundra to the north.

Precambrian Shield   Forbidding, barren, harsh – that's the Precambrian Shield. Underlying nearly half of Canada's area, and commonly called the Canadian Shield, this region surrounding Hudson Bay is named for its shape as well as for the pick-bending vigour of its bedrock.

The shield is noted for its innumerable lakes and rivers, its thin soil, and its sheer inhospitality – a combination of rock and bog makes most of it inaccessible. As much as a quarter of the world's fresh water is concentrated here.

Across the shield runs one of Canada's most distinctive features – a great crescent of boreal forest sweeping from Newfoundland to the Cordillera of British Columbia and the Yukon. Surviving the severe winters are conifers such as fir, pine, spruce, cedar and tamarack, as well as a few hardy species of broad-leaved deciduous trees such as birch and aspen. Many of Canada's mammals – including beavers, weasels, porcupines, wolves, moose and chipmunks – live in the boreal forest.

North of this forest is the broad transition zone called the tree line, beyond which low temperatures, short growing seasons and severe winters ensure that no trees are able to survive. These barren grounds are part of the tundra and taiga vegetation zone that extends north from the tree line to the uppermost reaches of Canada.

Great Lakes-St. Lawrence Lowlands   Sandwiched between the Canadian Shield and the Appalachians, and running along the northern coast of the greatest inland waterway in the world – the Great Lakes-St. Lawrence Seaway – is one of the most important industrial and agricultural belts of the continent, the Great Lakes-St. Lawrence Lowlands.

During the Paleozoic era (200 to 500 million years ago), great stretches of this region were submerged under the sea for long periods. Hundreds of metres of sand, silt and mud accumulated over the hard rocks of the shield, providing the basis for the lowlands' characteristic well-drained, rich agricultural soil.

Mixed forests once thrived in this soil, with trees close to the size of those of the British Columbia coast. In southwestern Ontario, hot summers and mild winters encouraged deciduous trees including walnut, elm, oak, maple, beech, chestnut, hickory and sassafras. The light soil also supported huge stands of white pine. These forests were largely cut down during the 17th, 18th and 19th centuries, as immigrants cleared the land for farming and settlement.

Appalachians   Two hundred million years ago, Europe and Northern Africa collided with North America, and the Appalachians were the first mountains to fold up on the edge of the continent. Since then, relentless erosion by glaciers, wind, rivers and sea has reduced them to plateaus and low rounded mountains – mere stumps of their former selves.

The Appalachian Mountains roll southeast from the St. Lawrence River across the Gaspé Peninsula and into New Brunswick, then head eastwards to the Atlantic – a total distance of about 600 kilometres. They end at the Nova Scotia coast with a craggy profile of capes, inlets, cliffs, and stretches of sandy beach. The bays and inlets have some of the fastest tides in the world.

The Appalachian area is mostly flat and rolling upland, with a few peaks rising no higher than 1 280 metres. Between these uplands are plains – notably Prince Edward Island and the Annapolis, Restigouche and Saint John River valleys – created by retreating glaciers depositing tremendously rich soil.

Much of the region is covered by a dense mixed forest of coniferous and deciduous trees.

T h e   H u m a n   L a n d s c a p e

Inhabitants of this country have always wrestled with the land. Ice Age Paleoindians would have starved had they not followed caribou herds across treacherous frozen wilderness. Pioneer farmers struggled against frost and drought, hail and wind, insects, weeds and disease – not to mention cabin fever. Even today, prospecting mining companies can spend up to six years – and $25 million – on planning and construction before finding ore.

And yet the land has always been generous in forests and food, as well as in minerals and fuels. With resources to spare, Canadians have traditionally sold their surplus to the world, using this income to buy goods from other countries.

Canada's First Peoples   During the closing phases of the last Ice Age – about 10,000 years ago – North America was joined to Asia by the Beringian Plain, which spanned what is now the Bering Strait. This expanse of continental shelf was exposed when continental glaciers trapped vast quantities of water, causing world sea levels to drop 100 metres or more below present levels.

Unlike most of North America, Eastern Asia was practically free of glaciers during the Ice Age, likely because of its dry climate. During interglacial periods, eastern Siberian hunters headed northwards in pursuit of animal herds that grazed the land now freed from continental glaciers. These animals included arctic-adapted species of bison, horse and camel, as well as giant ground sloths and beavers. The Stone Age hunters followed these animals across the Beringian Plain, and – without knowing it – stepped onto a new continent.

These first immigrants to the New World were the ancestors of North America's native peoples, whose history on the continent stretches back 20 times farther than that of European settlers.

The Northwest Territories   The Northwest Territories cover more than a third of Canada's area but contain less than 1% of its population. Historically, people living here have been either Inuit (formerly called ''Eskimos''), Dene or Métis Indians; more recent arrivals have come from elsewhere in Canada to work in government, services or mining.

For thousands of years, the lives of the nomadic Inuit revolved around hunting sea mammals, especially seals and whales. These provided food; oil for heat and light; skins for clothing, shelter and boats; and bone and ivory for harpoons and other tools. Today, the nomadic way of life has almost disappeared, although many Inuit still live by hunting, supplemented by sales of traditional arts and crafts. Despite the pervasiveness of modern culture in the North, the Inuit have retained more of their traditional ways than have most of North America's native peoples.

South of the Inuit lands, in the sub-Arctic, generation upon generation of Athapascan-speaking Dene Indians followed caribou herds and fished, living in cone-shaped lodges similar to teepees. Some of the Dene still follow a traditional way of life. Ever since the discovery of pitchblende and silver on the shores of Great Bear Lake in 1930, the Northwest Territories' economy has revolved around mining. In fact, the great gold discoveries of the 1930s at Yellowknife, the capital, are still mined today.

Celebrating, Canadian Style Nowhere is Canada's history, geography and multicultural heritage more evident than in its festivals. *

Northwest Territories and the Yukon
Midnight Golf Tournament, Yellowknife, June.

British Columbia
Gold Panning Days, Taylor, September.

Alberta
Ukrainian Pysanka Festival, Vegreville, July.

Saskatchewan
Sakimay Indian Powwow, Grenfell, June.

Manitoba
Islendingadagurinn, Gimli, August.

Ontario
Stratford Shakespeare Festival, Stratford, May-October.

Quebec
Carnaval de Québec, Quebec City, February.

Nova Scotia
Herring Choker's Picnic, Blandford, July.

New Brunswick
Loyalist Days, Saint John, July.

Prince Edward Island
Prince Edward Island Potato Blossom Festival, O'Leary, July.

Newfoundland
French Shore Shrimp Festival, Ingornachoix Bay, July.

* This is not a complete list of Canadian festivals.

Vast deposits of zinc and lead are mined at Pine Point on the Great Slave Lake, as well as at Nanisivik near Arctic Bay, and on Baffin Island.

Natural gas is extracted and processed at plants near Fort Liard, as is oil at Norman Wells on the Mackenzie River. The Mackenzie Delta-Beaufort Sea region and the High Arctic Islands are likely sources of major oil and gas fields, but pipelines or tanker routes through Arctic seas must be established before these resources can be tapped.

Fur trapping, forestry, tourism and the sale of native arts and crafts also contribute to the Northwest Territories' economy.

British Columbia and the Yukon   One grizzly bear for every four people, that's how low the population density is in the Yukon. British Columbia isn't much different. Two-thirds of its people live in the southwest corner of the province, with nearly half in Vancouver, which contains what is perhaps the most densely populated square kilometre in Canada.

The economies of British Columbia and the Yukon have always depended on natural resources. For thousands of years, West Coast tribes – including the Haida, the Cordillera Indians and the Athapascan-speaking tribes of the Yukon – hunted, fished and trapped this region. The Haida carved giant cedar trees into totem poles and forged one of North America's most elaborate native cultures.

About a quarter of North America's saleable timber is found in British Columbia, much of it in the rain-forest climate of the coastal region. Here, where thousand-year-old trees can be found, the forest industry is crucial. British Columbia has only 15% of Canada's total forest area, yet produces two-thirds of the country's sawn lumber, most of its plywood and a quarter of its chemical pulp.

Offshore, no fewer than 300 species of fish – as well as clams, oysters and crab – sustain a commercial fishery worth $285.6 million in 1991.

British Columbia's extensive minerals industry is dominated by metals and fuels. In the chief mining region, the Kootenays, lead, zinc and silver are extracted. As well, some of the largest deposits of soft coal in North America are mined here and then exported, mainly to Japan. Ninety percent of Canada's molybdenum (a metal used to strengthen steel) and 40% of its copper are found in the Highland Valley near Kamloops. Natural gas and oil are recovered from the Peace River area.

Hydroelectric power has boomed since the Second World War, with the W.A.C. Bennett Dam on the Peace River generating more than 30% of British Columbia's total.

With a smaller proportion of cultivated land than any other province except Newfoundland, British Columbia nevertheless generates 5% of Canada's agricultural output, helped by the longest growing season in the country. The Lower Fraser Valley is a land of dairy cattle and crops, and the great interior plateau, ''The Cariboo,'' is cattle-raising country. The Peace River area east of the Rockies is the province's chief grain-growing area,

while the Okanagan Valley contains 90% of British Columbia's orchards.

Thanks to the Alaska Highway, the Yukon has begun developing its vast reserves of zinc, lead, silver, cadmium, copper, tungsten and gold.

The Prairies   Duncan Macpherson, Canada's beloved editorial cartoonist, once described the Canadian prairie as ''one part horizon, nine parts sky.'' But although this flat-as-your-hand region has the reputation of being nothing but fields, fields, grain elevators and fields, its vastness is awe-inspiring – it covers more area than Mexico.

''Prairie'' comes from the French word for meadow, and originally referred to the large area of natural grassland in the centre of North America. Canadians say ''the Prairies'' to denote the three provinces – Alberta, Saskatchewan and Manitoba – in which this grassland was once located, even though much of the area was never true prairie.

The nomadic Blackfoot, Assiniboine, Cree, Sarcee and Gros Ventre Indian tribes and their predecessors were for 5,000 years the sole inhabitants of this region, hunting plains buffalo and living off little else. Early settlers and fur traders, helped by repeating rifles, decimated the buffalo herds by the 1880s. Much of the prairie was fenced, and cultivation began.

Today, the Prairies contain 80% of Canada's farmland. Grains are the main crop, with farmers here harvesting almost all of Canada's wheat – about 30 million tonnes every year. Canadians

The Exhilarating Prairies ''There is no more exhilarating sight in the west than the prospect of the binders at work on the sea-wide, sky-skirted prairie, with the golden grain gleaming under the August sun and above and about all the cloudless blue dome of heaven. And when the last sheaf has been cut and the binders are silent, how splendid is the view across the gently rolling stubble fields; stook beyond stook, stook beyond stook, for a quarter of a mile, for half a mile, and still more stooks as far as the eye can see, stooks cresting the horizon, ten thousand stooks all waiting to be threshed and each with its promise of bread, the gift of the New World to the Old.''

Reginald A. H. Buller. ''Wheat in the West''. 1924.

consume a quarter of this, and most of the rest is shipped to the European Economic Community, Japan, China and the Russian Federation.

This region also grows 90% of Canada's barley and rye, and more than 75% of its oats. Mustard and buckwheat are also common, as are peas, sunflowers and potatoes. In Saskatchewan, mixed farming is widespread, as are poultry, egg and livestock production.

Manitoba is farm country. It grows canola (rapeseed) and flax, as well as wheat and other grains. Other farms concentrate on raising beef cattle, with dairy farms clustering around Winnipeg.

Most of Canada's potash – the second-most valuable industrial mineral – is found in Saskatchewan. The province's reserves are estimated at roughly a quarter of the world's supply, and, at current rates of consumption, would last for 2,000 years.

To the west, in Alberta, wheat fields give way to cattle ranches, oilfields and mines. Extensive irrigation and nutritional native grasses make the dry southwest Canada's second-most important cattle-raising area, after British Columbia's Cariboo region. With more than 80% of Canada's oil reserves, Alberta supplies half of Canada's oil and gas and 90% of its natural gas from more than 130 fields. Edmonton, once a fur trading outpost, is now a major petrochemical centre. And Calgary, nicknamed ''Cowtown'' because of its ranching associations, is now headquarters for the nation's oil and gas industries. Even further

west, Alberta's foothills rise into the Rocky Mountains, where tourism is the major industry of the beautiful national parks of Banff and Jasper.

Boreal forest and tundra stretch across the top of all three provinces, covering nearly half of their total area. This harsh region is home to remote communities based on forestry and mining.

Central Region   Canada's Central Region is so named not because it sits in the middle of the country but because it is Canada's industrial and economic heartland. Fully 60% of Canadians live in the 5% of the country taken up by the Great Lakes-St. Lawrence Lowlands running through Ontario and Quebec.

The Central Region's vitality stems largely from cheap water transportation along the lakes, rivers and canals that make up the Great Lakes-St. Lawrence Seaway. The locks at Sault Ste. Marie, a major steel-producing area, are busier than the Panama Canal.

Before the arrival of white settlers, northern Ontario and Quebec were inhabited by nomadic Indians of the sub-Arctic culture. Further south were the Eastern Woodlands Indians of the Algonkian and Iroquoian language groups. These tribes were semi-sedentary; they cultivated beans, corn and squash, moving on every 10 years or so when the soil was exhausted.

Farming has been practiced in the Central Region ever since, and still thrives today thanks to the fertile soils and a moist climate.

Per Capita Energy Use
G-7 Countries, 1991

Canada

United States

W. Germany

United Kingdom

France

Japan

```
          2      4      6      8      10
```

(tonnes of oil equivalent)

Source:
Organization for Economic
Co-operation and Development, 1991

Major crops are field corn and soybeans, followed by sweet corn, tomatoes and other vegetables.

The section of the Niagara Peninsula on the shores of Lake Ontario is one of Canada's most important fruit-growing regions. Here summer workers support the seasonal economy by picking peaches, cherries and strawberries, as well as grapes for the region's wine-making industry.

Dairy farming and cheese and butter production are the predominant industries around Montreal and in the southeastern corner of Ontario, and other livestock are raised in the Georgian Bay-Upper Grand River region.

No other part of Canada produces more minerals than Ontario. This wealth includes nickel, gold, silver, platinum, uranium, zinc and copper, as well as a range of structural materials. Ontario is important for salt and gypsum, and produces more non-fuel minerals for commercial use than any other province.

Most of these minerals are dug out of the vast reserves of the Canadian Shield. The Sudbury Basin, for example, is the largest productive area for nickel in the world, accounting for 70% of Canada's total production, most of which is exported to the United States.

Forestry, fishing, fur production and hydroelectricity also add considerably to Ontario's economy. Pulp, paper and sawn lumber are its main forestry products; the province ranks third after British Columbia and Quebec in value of production. Thanks to the Great Lakes, Ontario leads Canada in the value of fish taken from inland waters. Fur production – the province's oldest industry – still supports trappers and fur farmers. Ontario's thundering rivers ensure that the province ranks third after Quebec and British Columbia in exploited hydroelectric power.

Half of Quebec's vast forests can be converted into saleable forest products, and three-quarters of this softwood is suitable for making pulp and paper. Quebec leads Canada in this industry, producing about a third of the country's total. If newsprint is included, Quebec produces half of Canada's total pulp and paper – 20% of the world's supply.

As with Ontario, Quebec's mineral wealth comes from the Canadian Shield. It includes large deposits of copper, and smaller quantities of gold, silver, zinc, lead and nickel. Estrie, formerly the Eastern Townships, sits above vast asbestos reserves; more than 80% of Canada's chrysotile asbestos comes from Quebec.

Atlantic Region   Inhabitants of Canada's Atlantic Region have a profound and enduring obsession with the sea. Prince Edward Islanders – famous for their potatoes – nickname their home "Spud Island." And to Nova Scotians and Newfoundlanders the sea is both a blessing and a curse, since – as the locals say – Nova Scotia is "a peninsula entirely surrounded by fish," while Newfoundland is simply "a piece of rock entirely surrounded by fog."

Long before these nicknames were coined, the Atlantic Region was inhabited by Eastern Woodlands Indians – mostly Malecites, who cultivated the land in southern New Brunswick, and Micmacs, who hunted and fished throughout the region.

Fishing is still a primary industry, although many fish stocks are declining. Giant bluefin tuna are still caught off the coasts of all four provinces, and other popular catches include Prince Edward Island's famous Malpeque oysters and New Brunswick's sardines. Atlantic salmon is also popular, as are Nova Scotia's Digby scallops, shrimps, clams, and crab. The most valuable catch, however, is lobster.

The submerged continental shelf off Newfoundland's south and east coasts – the ''Grand Banks'' of Newfoundland – provides the world's most extensive breeding grounds for fish. Cod was once so abundant here that islanders simply called it ''fish.''

Agriculture is important in the three Maritime Provinces (Prince Edward Island, Nova Scotia, New Brunswick), particularly in the Saint John River Valley of New Brunswick (potatoes and livestock) and the Annapolis Valley of Nova Scotia (famous for its fruit, mainly apples).

Potatoes are to Prince Edward Island what wheat is to Saskatchewan, largely because of the island's silty, stone-free soils. Prince Edward Island and New Brunswick produce 90% of Canada's domestic seed potatoes and the majority of the country's potato exports.

In Nova Scotia, the land supports dairy farming and poultry production. In New Brunswick, potato, livestock, and mixed farming are important.

Mining is significant in New Brunswick. Zinc, lead and copper are mined near Bathurst, antimony around Fredericton and potash near Sussex. Northeastern New Brunswick's forests are threaded by famous rivers – the Miramichi, the Restigouche and the Matapedia – that feed millions of logs downstream to sawmills and pulp companies.

New Brunswick is also the only Atlantic province with significant hydroelectric power resources, mainly on the Saint John River. Innovators in Nova Scotia are operating North America's first experimental tidal power generating station on the Bay of Fundy, harnessing some of the most powerful tides in the world.

Newfoundland and Labrador's once-dominant fishery has been surpassed in recent years by forestry and mining since completion of the Trans-Canada Highway across the island. Pulp and paper manufacturing has increased greatly, as has mining of iron ore, lead, zinc, copper, gold, silver, asbestos and gypsum.

Newfoundlanders are awaiting developments in marine oil and gas technology before tapping the island's considerable offshore oil and natural gas reserves.

Canada's Climate

Canada's size and diversity produce a kaleidoscope of most of the climates of the Western Hemisphere – everything from the cold and snow of Siberia to the summer heat and humidity of the Caribbean. Canada is a land of climatic contrasts and extremes. We have it all!

The North   Every June in Canada's North, where the mid-summer sun never really sets, golfers from around the world gather to compete in the City of Yellowknife's famous golf tournament. Summers in the North being bright but short, the contestants make the most of it – the tee-off is just after midnight.

Summer over, both golfers and citizens move inside. In the Canadian North, winter is simply long, white, dark and cold. The mercury drops below –18°C for five months or more, and the annual range of temperatures is one of the greatest in North America. Here are generated the frigid Arctic air masses that descend over much of North America every winter, occasionally reaching the tip of the Florida Keys.

Annual precipitation is so low that large parts of the North would be desert were it not for the permafrost that keeps the surface moist. Yellowknife receives 25 centimetres or less of precipitation per year, and the North overall – despite popular perceptions – gets less snow than any other province or territory.

British Columbia   The sweater-or-swimming-trunks diversity of Canada's climates is nowhere more striking than in British Columbia. Here are thundering rivers and parched valleys; Mediterranean mildness and foggy coasts; damp Pacific rain forests and snowy plains; snow-capped peaks and the balmy Gulf Islands. British Columbia's climates are so extreme that residents of Vancouver can play golf and go skiing – on the same midwinter day.

Our Weather: Exciting, But Not the Most Extreme

Hottest:
45°C, Midale and Yellow Grass, Sask., July 5, 1937.
58°C, Al'azizyah, Libya, September 13, 1922.

Coldest:
–63°C, Snag, Yukon Territory, February 3, 1947.
–89.6°C, Vostok, Antarctica, July 21, 1983.

Driest:
12.7 mm, Arctic Bay, Northwest Territories, 1949.
0.0 mm, Arica, Chile – no rain for 14 years.

Rainiest Day:
489.2 mm, Ucluelet, Brynnor Mines, B.C., October 6, 1967.
1 869.9 mm, Cilaos, La Réunion Island, March 15, 1952.

Sea Smoke The waters off Newfoundland's Avalon Peninsula and over the Grand Banks are among the foggiest in the world. ''Sea smoke'' develops when warm, humid air from the south mixes with air over the frigid, sometimes ice-infested waters of the Labrador Current. These fogs also invade Halifax, Nova Scotia, which gets about 122 days of pea-soup visibility per year.

Winters along the West Coast, because of the generally warm and always ice-free waters of the Pacific Ocean, are the mildest in the country; summers are comfortably warm. Winter brings plenty of rain and drizzle, and the mountain slopes are the wettest sites in Canada. ''If you can see the mountains,'' say the locals, ''it's going to rain. If you can't see them, it's already raining.''

This oceanic climate does not affect much of the rest of Canada, though, because the Cordillera Mountains impede the eastward penetration of the low-level, moist Pacific air streams.

Four hundred kilometres inland, between the Coast Mountains and the Rockies, the climate is continental. Cold Arctic air spills between the Rockies from the Prairies, making winters cold. Further south, in the rainshadow of the Coast Mountains, are some of the most arid areas in the country.

The northern half of the province experiences a combination of Arctic and Pacific weather systems, and is characterized by long, cold winters and short, cool summers. Many of the western slopes and mountain peaks receive more than 400 centimetres of snow a year.

The Prairies   In 1882, the *Settler's Guide to the North-West* was candid: ''The climate of Manitoba consists of seven months of Arctic weather and five months of cold weather.'' Weather records show that children in Manitoba have had snowball fights during every month but July. This is largely because the Prairie Provinces have the most extreme continental climate in Canada – and the most unpredictable.

The Prairies, having no high mountains, are open to Arctic winds in winter and hot, dry southern air in summer. They are also in the heartland of the continent, far from the influence of oceans. Consequently, the Prairie Provinces, especially in the agricultural south, experience sudden weather changes and incredible annual temperature ranges – sometimes greater than 50°C.

Prairie winters are long and cold, though bright and crisp; summers are short and hot with little humidity – perfect for growing high-quality grain. Precipitation is low, and frequently arrives as blizzards in winter and violent thunderstorms in summer. In some years, a lack of precipitation, combined with hot summer temperatures and wind, has produced severe droughts.

Central Region   Montreal, located in the heart of Central Canada, gets more snow than any other major world city. About 40 million tonnes descend every winter, costing the city about $45 million in street clearing expenses alone. Removing 40 million tonnes of snow is the equivalent of towing away 200,000 compact cars a day for seven months!

Southwest of Montreal, the Great Lakes, with their water volume of 23 000 cubic kilometres, act as a vast heat reservoir, modifying the weather of southern Ontario and southern Quebec. The Great Lakes keep winter temperatures mild compared with the rest of Canada. The 220-day growing season permits corn to grow almost as well as it does in the American Middle West. Peaches, apples and grapes are grown commercially on the shores of Lake Erie and Lake Ontario.

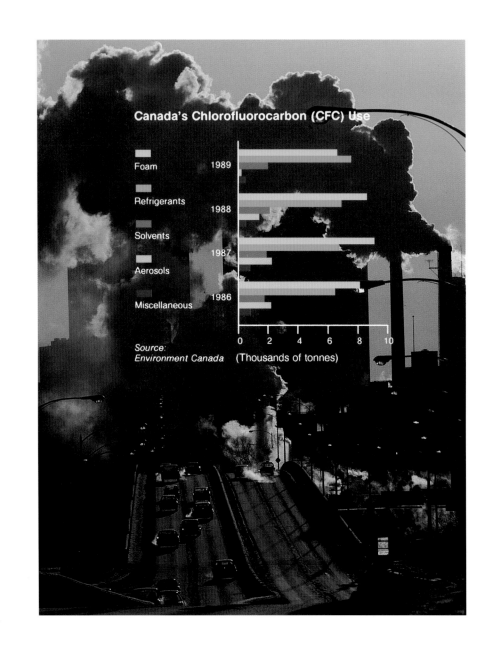

When winter's cold air is warmed several degrees by the open water, the atmosphere is fed large amounts of moisture, some of which falls as "lake-effect" snow south of the Great Lakes. In fall, the stored heat of summer delays the first frost by one or two weeks within 10 to 15 kilometres of the shoreline.

Atlantic Region   Nor'easters, silver thaws and sea smoke – that's what the inhabitants of the Atlantic Region call the storms, freezing rain and dense fog that characterize their part of Canada. Newfoundlanders are fond of telling visitors that their province has two seasons – August and winter.

Packing everything from heavy precipitation to hurricane-force winds and blizzards, nor'easters can pass rapidly over the region or stall and batter it for days. Always hardest hit is the Atlantic Coast of Nova Scotia, which gets more storms than any other area of Canada. Newfoundland as a whole receives the strongest winds of any province, with average wind speeds greater than 20 kilometres per hour. Prince Edward Island is also vulnerable to volatile weather systems originating in the North Pacific and the Gulf of Mexico, making its winters stormy and unpredictable.

Freezing rainstorms often paralyze the Atlantic Region for days in winter, damaging trees and property, powerlines and vehicles, and disrupting transportation and other essential services. A four-day storm in April of 1984 blanketed St. John's, Newfoundland, with ice that was 15 centimetres thick in places.

Summers here are warm and sunny, with Chatham, New Brunswick, recording an average of 2,000 hours of sunshine a year. Warm temperatures encourage the region's agricultural industries, and help to attract tourists to the area's many beaches, particularly those of Prince Edward Island.

Environmental Issues

Polluted waterways, city smog and contaminated groundwater and soil are just a few of the signs that Canada's natural heritage is endangered. And global threats such as climate change, ozone depletion and acid rain show that pollution does not respect international boundaries.

Increasing concern over the environment is prompting Canadians to change how they think and act. Individuals, businesses, government – all are helping to solve the problems threatening Canada and the world.

Climate Change   When humans burn fossil fuels or deforest large areas, "greenhouse" gases – particularly carbon dioxide (CO_2) – accumulate in the atmosphere. These gases trap heat radiating from the earth's surface, gradually warming the climate. Most of the CO_2 emitted in human history has been in this century, and as a result average global temperatures have risen 0.5°C. Unless greenhouse gas emissions are reduced considerably, average temperatures could rise another 3°C by the year 2100.

For Canada, global warming could mean a much drier climate, severely affecting agriculture, forestry and water supply. The risks of fire and coastal flooding could increase.

Canada is committed to stabilizing emissions of carbon dioxide and other greenhouse gases at 1990 levels by the year 2000.

Ozone Depletion   Another major global problem is thinning of the ozone layer – a fragile band of gases in the upper atmosphere that absorbs most of the sun's harmful ultraviolet radiation. Caused mostly by chlorofluorocarbons (CFCs) – chemicals used in refrigeration, air conditioning and foam packaging – ozone thinning increases the earth's ultraviolet exposure. This in turn could lead to more skin cancer, and threatens Canada's crops, forests and offshore fisheries.

As a signatory to the United Nations' Montreal Protocol, Canada pledges to phasing out CFCs by 1997.

Acid Rain   Acid rain, caused by emissions of sulphur dioxide (SO_2) and nitrogen oxide, damages lakes and forests. Reducing Canada's acid rain problem means reducing acid deposition originating in both Canada and the United States by about half. In 1991, the Canada-United States Air Quality Agreement established this reduction as a goal for 1994.

Urban Air Quality   Thanks to tougher motor vehicle emission standards and a ban on leaded gasoline, Canadians are breathing cleaner air in the 1990s. However, ground-level ozone, a component of smog, is still a problem – over half of Canadians in urban areas are exposed to unhealthy ozone levels.

In 1990, the provinces and the federal government embarked on a 15-year strategy to reduce ozone concentrations.

Solid Waste   Canada produces more garbage per capita than any other country. Every day, the average Canadian throws out about 1.8 kilograms of residential waste. Not surprisingly, municipalities across the country are running out of landfill space.

Faced with this problem, Canadians have begun to work vigorously to reduce solid waste. Municipal composting and recycling programs are becoming common, and consumers are demanding less product packaging. Some experts have even suggested generating energy by burning waste – but this could produce carbon emissions and other hazardous byproducts.

Endangered Wildlife   Canada's wildlife habitats are vanishing at an alarming rate. Particularly vulnerable are wetlands, home to a remarkable range of plant and animal species. Already 20 million hectares of Canadian wetlands have been destroyed, threatening waterfowl that use them for breeding and wintering.

About 7% of Canada's land and freshwater area is totally or partially protected in national and provincial parks, national wildlife areas and bird sanctuaries. Canada's goal is to protect 12% of its land and freshwater areas by the year 2000.

*M*y vision of Canada has all my life been determined by my first twelve years on the Saskatchewan billiard table south of

Regina. All that land and all that sky taught me early that to be human means to be conscious of self. Such separation from

all the rest of the living whole had a high price: Billy Mitchell was mortal; he could die. This insight has been very helpful in

deciding what is important and what is unimportant, valuable. It also made me very aware of my inner self.

Like others in Mid-America, on the moors of England, the steppes of Russia, it made me a writer.

W.O. Mitchell, Alberta novelist and playwright, Member of the Order of Canada and recipient of the Leacock Medal for Humour.

THE PEOPLE

In a speech given several months before his death in 1991, Canadian literary critic Northrop Frye noted that Canada preserves its identity by having many identities.

Indeed, diversity is the heart and soul of Canada. Canadians speak French, English, Urdu, Spanish, Chinese and dozens of other languages. We practice Christianity, Buddhism, Judaism, Islam and a host of other religions – or no religion at all. We may wear suits, dresses, chadors, turbans or caftans. And we may eat moussaka, curry or tabouli, in addition to more standard Canadian fare.

Some Canadians live on farms, some in small towns, others in large cities. Many Canadians live alone; a growing number live in common-law unions; many more live in one-parent families, double-income families and "blended" families encompassing children from previous marriages.

In 1991, this diversity was shared by 27.3 million Canadians, according to Statistics Canada population counts – eight times the 1867 total of 3.4 million. Canada's diversity may continue to grow, but its population may not. In fact, a decline could start just after the turn of the century. The cause would be Canada's low fertility rate: Canadians are not having enough children to maintain the population. Current immigration levels may delay the decline, but cannot stop it. Experts say that if current trends continue Canada's population may peak at just under 30 million around 2025, eventually stabilizing at close to 18 million, a level Canada first reached in the late 1950s.

The decline in Canada's population is just one of many changes that may alter the country's social fabric. The proportion of seniors in Canada's population could double within 40 years. More Canadians are likely to live alone. And immigration will continue adding to our kaleidoscope of cultures and customs. Indeed, as Canada enters the 21st century, perhaps the only certainty, as Mr. Frye suggested, is diversity. Canadian society will likely encompass new types of living arrangements, lifestyles and beliefs, remaining one of the most dynamic countries on earth.

This chapter explores the demographic terrain of Canada: the mix of languages, religions, family types and peoples that form the country's identity, and the trends that may shape its future. In addition, it features brief profiles of the 10 provinces and the Yukon and the Northwest Territories.

For many of the subjects covered, this chapter uses data from the 1991 Census. However, at the time of publication, not all 1991 Census data had been released; in some cases, 1986 or 1981 census data were the most current available.

The Immigrant Experience

A hundred years ago, thousands of immigrants to Canada began their new lives in a sod hut on a windswept prairie. In the harsh, crude conditions of the frontier, the first few years of the pioneer's life were a struggle to survive. As one early settler lamented,

"Lord, have compassion upon me, a poor unfortunate sinner, three thousand miles from my own country, and seventy-five from anywhere else."

Today, most immigrants face different challenges. For these new Canadians, the rigours of homesteading have been replaced by the demands of a modern society. Their first steps on Canadian soil are frequently on an airport tarmac and their first home is often in a high-rise apartment. Often they must learn one or both of Canada's official languages, adjust to Canadian customs and culture, gain an understanding of Canadian law, and find work and a place to live. Yet like Canada's early pioneers, most immigrants adapt quickly to Canadian life, and their contributions energize the nation's economy and society.

Since becoming a nation in 1867, Canada has had two periods of particularly intensive immigration: 1901 to 1931, and 1951 to 1981. In each period, Canada accepted more than 4 million immigrants.

For most of Canada's history, the majority of immigrants came from Europe and the United States. This changed radically in the 1960s, when merit became the main criterion for selecting immigrants. In 1991, Canada's immigrants came from more than 150 countries, with more than 70% from Asia, Africa and Latin America; less than 25% were from Europe and the United States.

Today the average age of an immigrant to Canada is 27 – compared with a national average of just over 30 – and he or she tends to be more highly skilled or better educated than the average native-born Canadian. Fairly equal numbers of men and women are now accepted.

Most immigrants tend to settle in one of three provinces: Ontario, Quebec or British Columbia. Like native-born Canadians, immigrants tend to follow the jobs, so they often head to larger cities. About 35% of immigrants are destined for Toronto, another 14% for Montreal and 11% for Vancouver.

Immigrants make a strong economic contribution to Canada. They start businesses, they invest, they buy goods and services. In 1988 alone, immigrants collectively injected more than $4.5 billion into Canada. Immigrants are also less likely than native-born Canadians to receive social assistance, and with their generally high skill and education levels, they bring professional expertise. Because their average incomes are higher, they tend to contribute more in taxes.

The 1986 Census found that 4 million Canadians, or 16% of the population, were not born in this country. In the United States, 6% of the population are foreign-born; in France, 11%; and in Australia, 22%. Many Canadians are visible minorities – 6.3% in 1986. The share is even higher in Canada's major cities – 17% in Toronto and Vancouver, 10% in Calgary and Edmonton, and 7% in Montreal.

Since the early 1970s, the Canadian government has followed a policy of multiculturalism, which encourages all Canadians to preserve and build on their cultural heritages. Despite this

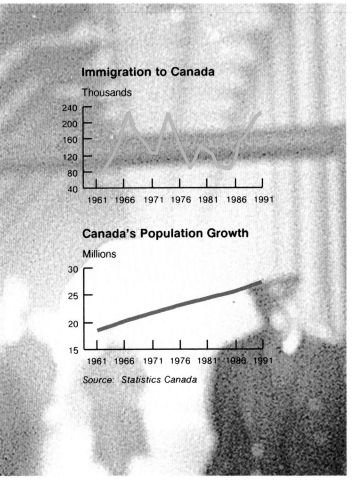

Immigration to Canada

Thousands

240
200
160
120
80
40

1961　1966　1971　1976　1981　1986　1991

Canada's Population Growth

Millions

30

25

20

15

1961　1966　1971　1976　1981　1986　1991

Source: Statistics Canada

policy, incidents of racism and intolerance still occur in Canada. One of the great challenges for Canada is to eliminate this discrimination, allowing all Canadians equal participation in their society.

The Changing Canadian Family

In the 1800s, most Canadians lived and worked on small family farms, and most businesses were family run. Without safety nets such as welfare or unemployment insurance, Canadians depended for support on one another, on the community and on religious institutions. Extended families – in which children, parents and close relatives such as grandparents all lived under one roof – were common.

But radical changes in Canada's economic conditions have altered the shape of families and their role in society. In fact, the so-called traditional family – the mother at home, the father in the work force, the children at school – was common only from the end of World War Two to the early 1960s. Today, Canadian families may be headed by working parents, by lone parents, by parents "living together," by grandparents, or even by parents who have children from previous marriages.

A generation ago, families of three, four and five children were common: today, many couples have one or no children. In 1991, the average family had 3.1 members, down from 3.9 in 1961. Families are getting smaller partly because of the rise in one-parent families, but the most important reason is the declining fertility rate – Canadians are having fewer children.

In 1989, Statistics Canada tracked a fertility rate just above 1.7 children per woman; this is a sharp drop from a rate of 3.5 in 1951, and well below the crucial mark of 2.1 needed to maintain today's population. Indeed, if immigration ceased and Canada's fertility rate stayed at 1.7, the last Canadian would die about 800 years from now.

Many Canadians assume that the decline in fertility is recent; in fact, it began about 120 years ago, although temporary upswings occurred in the late 1930s and during the "baby boom" from the late 1940s to the early 1960s. Today, Canada's fertility rate is higher than that of most other developed western countries.

One of the most striking recent changes in Canadian society is the rise of double-income families – families in which both spouses work. In the early 1960s, most families were "traditional" – a husband and wife, with only the husband working. Today, the double-income family is the norm.

The share of one-parent families has also risen in recent years – to 13% of families in 1991, up from about 10% in 1971. The leading reason for one-parent families is divorce (29.9%), followed by separation (29.6%), widowhood (27%) and births to unmarried women (13.4%). Most one-parent families are led by women, and increasingly, by young women aged 15 to 34. One-parent families are more likely to have lower incomes

and to need social assistance; hence children of such families often have poorer health care, education, housing and recreation. Frequently, these families do not receive ''child support'' payments from the absent spouse. The emotional burden on single parents can be high: generally, they report being less happy than other Canadians, according to a 1985 Statistics Canada survey.

Marriage and Divorce

Divorce, the chief reason for the increase in one-parent families, now affects one-third of all Canadian marriages. Canada's divorce rate began to skyrocket after legislation in 1968 made divorce easier to obtain. Compared with other western industrialized countries, however, Canada's rate is moderate. In 1990, the divorce rate was 416.3 divorces per 1,000 marriages – that's almost three times the 1969 rate (143.3). The peak was 499.9 per 1,000 in 1987.

Many divorced Canadians remarry. In fact, in more than 40% of marriages in 1990, at least one spouse had been married before. This trend has led to a rise in ''blended'' families encompassing children from previous marriages.

Couples living together in common-law unions before marrying – or instead of marrying – became popular in Canada after 1970. Many young Canadians consider living together a necessary step toward marriage. In 1991, about 5.5% of adult Canadians were living together. In 1990, 28% of all Canadians aged 18 to 64 had lived common-law at least once. Common-law unions are most common among women in their 20s and men in their late 20s and early 30s.

More Canadians are divorcing or living together, but marriage is still overwhelmingly popular in Canada. In 1985, Statistics Canada estimated that about 85% of Canadians would marry at least once. However, Canadians now tend to marry later in life. In 1990, the average age at first marriage was almost 26.0 for women and almost 27.9 for men. In the 1950s and 1960s, Canadians married much younger – an average of 22.5 years for women and 25.0 for men.

Because the vast majority of Canadians marry, the two-parent family still predominates. But today's parents are more likely to share child-rearing and housekeeping than were parents a generation ago, when the burden fell almost completely on women. This shift has occurred because more women are working – by 1991, more than 58.2% of women aged 15 and older were in the labour force, up from 35.4% in 1966.

Growing Older

Canada's baby-boom generation makes up about one-third of the population – about 9 million Canadians. Born between 1947 and 1966 – at a rate of 400,000 to 500,000 per year – the boomers now range in age from 25 to 44. Because of their

Canada's Place in an Aging World
(Population Aged 65+)

Sweden (1988)

W. Germany (1990)

United Kingdom (1990)

France (1990)

United States (1990)

Japan (1990)

Canada (1990)

Czechoslovakia (1987)

Brazil (1980)

0   5   10   15   20
(Percentage)

Source:
United Nations, Demographic Handbook, 1991

numbers, they have profoundly influenced society. As children, they flooded the educational system, and many new schools were built to accommodate them. Later, they spurred Canada's expanding university system. As adults, their needs have influenced everything from product marketing strategies to rising house prices.

Early in the next century, boomers will start turning in briefcases, uniforms and work boots. Collectively, their retirement from the workforce will speed the aging of Canada's population. In 1991, 11.6% of Canadians were aged 65 and older. By the year 2031, the percentage of seniors could climb to 22%.

Canada's population is aging because we are having fewer children, which means that young people make up a shrinking share of the population. At the same time, both men and women are living longer. Health care continues to improve, and Canadians are eating better, exercising more, and smoking and drinking less.

But Canada is not aging "evenly." In the Yukon and the Northwest Territories, residents are, on average, much younger: less than 4% were seniors in 1991. But in Prince Edward Island, Manitoba, Saskatchewan and British Columbia, residents are older, on average, with seniors composing more than 12% of the population. If these provinces were countries, their populations would be among the world's most mature.

Other western countries also have aging populations. In Sweden, 17% of the population are seniors, a level Canada won't reach for another 20 to 30 years. Germany, France, the United Kingdom, Czechoslovakia and the United States are also "older" than Canada, although Canada is catching up.

Canada is young compared with other highly industrialized societies, but it is old compared to developing countries. For example, in Mexico, Brazil, the Philippines and Zaire, seniors make up less than 5% of the population.

Canada: Many Peoples, Many Languages

Today, most Canadians speak one or both of Canada's official languages, English and French. In 1986, English was the mother tongue – the language first learned and still understood – for 61% of Canadians. Another 24% spoke French as their mother tongue, and 16% could converse in either language. Only 1.1% of the population could not speak English or French.

The first languages spoken in Canada were those of the aboriginal peoples. These ancient languages have evolved over thousands of years and reflect the close ties aboriginal peoples have to the natural world.

In fact, the European explorers who first met the Inuit of Canada's North were astonished by the Inuit ability to navigate the tundra's featureless terrain of snow and ice. Because Inuit survival depended on intimate knowledge of the land, they easily identified landmarks invisible to untrained European eyes. This detailed knowledge was incorporated into the Inuit language,

City Life In 1851, only 13% of Canadians lived in urban areas. Since then, this share has constantly increased. In 1986, more than three out of four Canadians lived in urban areas – cities, towns, villages, hamlets, reserves and other centres of 1,000 people or more with a population density of at least 400 per square kilometre. Ontario was the most highly urbanized part of Canada (82.6%) and Prince Edward Island was the least – close to two-thirds of Prince Edward Islanders live in rural areas. Toronto, Montreal and Vancouver – the nation's largest metropolitan centres – account for just under one-third of Canada's population. Three-quarters of Canadians live within 150 kilometres of the Canada-U.S. border.

Inuktitut, which has more than a dozen words for types of snow. These include drifting snow (*natiruvaaq*); compact, damp snow (*kinirtaq*); melting snow (*mannguq*); and thawed snow that has refrozen with an ice surface (*qiasuqaq*).

Inuktitut is just one of dozens of languages developed by Canada's aboriginal peoples. Only 53 aboriginal languages survive. Of these, several are on the verge of extinction. For example, only a few hundred people still speak the West Coast languages of Haida, Tlingit and Kutenain. Although about 138,000 Canadians, or 0.6% of the population, spoke aboriginal languages in 1986, only three languages seem secure: Cree, Ojibwa and Inuktitut.

Canadians speak many other languages. The 1986 Census showed that Canada's most common non-official languages are Italian and Chinese, each spoken at home by about 250,000 Canadians, or about 1% of the population. German, Portuguese, Greek, Spanish, Polish and Ukrainian were each spoken by less than 1% of Canadians.

Some non-official languages are more common than others, depending on where you go in Canada. In Newfoundland, Nova Scotia, New Brunswick, the Yukon and the Northwest Territories, aboriginal languages are the main non-official languages. In Prince Edward Island, Dutch predominates; in Quebec, Greek; and in Ontario, German. Ukrainian and German are most common in Manitoba, Saskatchewan and Alberta, while Chinese leads in British Columbia.

In Newfoundland, English is the mother tongue for almost everyone – 98.8% of the population. Quebec is the only province with a French majority (82.8%); New Brunswick has the largest French minority (33.5%). In the rest of Canada, French is the mother tongue for less than 6% of the population.

Almost nine in 10 bilingual Canadians live in Quebec, Ontario or New Brunswick. In Quebec – by far the most bilingual province – the share of French-speakers is climbing steadily. In the rest of the country, the share of English-speakers is rising.

Most Canadians whose mother tongue is neither English nor French live in Toronto, Montreal and Vancouver. This is not surprising; most immigrants settle in these cities. Thus in 1986, a language other than English or French was the mother tongue for about 13% of Montreal's population, compared with 1.5% for the rest of Quebec; Toronto's share was 26.3%, compared with 10.9% for the rest of Ontario; and Vancouver's share was 21.3%, compared with 11.8% for the rest of British Columbia.

R e l i g i o n

In Canada, there are churches, mosques, synagogues and temples – but attendance in these places of worship is dropping. From 1961 to 1981, the percentage of Canadians with no religious affiliation climbed from 1% to 7.3%. Religious affiliation is lowest in British Columbia; in 1981, 20.5% of its population had none, compared with only 1% in Newfoundland.

On the Move In the five years between each census, almost half of Canadians pack up their bags and boxes and call the movers. In fact, Canadians are among the most enthusiastic movers in the world. Changing residence often means changing province. In 1986, 15% of Canadians no longer lived in the province where they were born, and 4% had changed provinces in the previous five years. In 1990, most interprovincial migrants were headed to Ontario, British Columbia and Alberta. However, the migrant traffic moves both ways; in Ontario, for example, more people moved out than moved in. Only Alberta, British Columbia and the Yukon gained overall.

Most of Canada's early immigrants came from the Christian countries of Europe, and so Canada is today overwhelmingly Christian. Indeed, almost 90% of Canadians stated Christianity as their religion in 1981.

In the early days, European settlers and missionaries converted many aboriginal peoples to Christianity. However, today aboriginal peoples across the country are reclaiming and strengthening their spiritual traditions. They have revived sweat lodges, spirit dances and fasting. Many elements of traditional religion have also been preserved in native Christian practice. Immigrants from regions such as Asia, Africa and the Middle East have introduced Judaism, Buddhism, Hinduism, Islam, Sikhism, the Baha'i faith and many other belief systems. More recently, some Canadians have turned to religions promoting self-awareness through a range of spiritual disciplines. These religions include Hare Krishna, Dharmadatu, Transcendental Meditation and Sri Chimnoy.

The First Nations: Canada's Aboriginal Peoples

Many native cultures explain the creation of the world with a story of twin brothers. One brother tries to make a paradise for humans, but the other brother undoes much of this work. The result is an imperfect world – the world we humans live in. In many ways this myth reflects the current situation of Canada's aboriginal peoples, who have confronted problems such as high unemployment and chronic poverty. But as Cree playwright Tomson Highway has said: ''Shamans have predicted that the native people will undergo a resurgence seven lifetimes after Columbus. That time has arrived…We no longer see the necessity of continuing as an oppressed people; we see a bright future ahead of us.''

At the time of European contact, distinct Indian nations lived throughout what is now Canada. Together, these nations may have numbered about 350,000 people. By 1867, they were decimated by starvation, war and disease and their numbers had dropped to less than 140,000. Since the 1920s, however, the aboriginal population has actually grown at a faster rate than the population at large. By 1991, about 830,000 Canadians, or 3% of the population, were of aboriginal origin, according to estimates from Indian and Northern Affairs Canada (INAC).

Canada's Constitution defines aboriginals as Indians, Inuits and Métis (persons of mixed white – usually French – and Indian ancestry). However, most federal programs for Canada's aboriginals apply only to status Indians – Indians registered under the Indian Act – and to Inuits. In 1991, INAC estimated there were about 423,000 status Indians (60% living on reserves) 215,000 non-status Indians, 160,000 Métis and 38,000 Inuit. Unemployment, one-parent families, crime, illness, alcoholism, poverty and high mortality – especially for infants – are all more common for aboriginals than for other Canadians.

Perhaps the most alarming statistic is the high aboriginal suicide

rate – twice the national average for status Indians and more than three times the national average for Inuits. Violent death – including death by fire and firearms – is also much more common among native Canadians, partly because many native communities have substandard housing and heating systems, little or no fire-fighting equipment, and high rates of gun ownership.

Canada's aboriginals – especially those living on reserves and in the North – tend to have more crowded housing than other Canadians. In 1986, less than 2% of all Canadian dwellings were crowded (more than one person per room), compared to almost one in 10 aboriginal dwellings. On reserves, the figure rose to almost three in 10, and for Inuit dwellings it was about one in three.

Most aboriginals live in rural or remote areas of the country. And aboriginal women have more children than do other Canadian women – hence aboriginals are becoming a larger share of Canada's population. High fertility rates also mean that young people are a larger portion of the aboriginal population than of the general population.

Canada's native peoples are now undergoing what might be called a social and spiritual renaissance. In the last 30 years, life expectancy has soared, while mortality has plunged. And in the 1980s and 1990s, many native political leaders, artists and writers achieved national prominence. Today, native communities across Canada are using ancient spiritual practices to solve modern problems. For example, traditional healing ceremonies and rituals have helped many bands and tribes to halt alcohol and drug abuse.

Provincial and Territorial Snapshots

Northwest Territories
- Population, 1991: 57,649
- Population by mother tongue, 1986: English, 55.3%; French, 2.7%; Other, 42%
- Proportion urban, 1986: 46.3%
- Area (square kilometres): 3,426,320

The N.W.T. is the only part of Canada with an aboriginal majority – in 1986, almost 60% of the population were of aboriginal descent. It also leads the country with its share of female one-parent families. Living common-law is popular here; more than 22% of families were common-law in 1991 – that is the highest rate in Canada. The N.W.T. has the ''youngest'' population in Canada – less than 3% are over age 65. It also has the highest fertility rate in the country – almost three children per woman in 1989.

Yukon
- Population, 1991: 27,797
- Population by mother tongue, 1986: English, 89.1%; French, 2.6%; Other, 8.3%
- Proportion urban, 1986: 64.7%

- Area (square kilometres): 483,450

Many small cities in Canada have larger populations than the entire Yukon, where people outnumber grizzly bears by a mere four-to-one ratio. The territory has a large aboriginal minority – 20% of the population in 1986. Today, six groups of Athapaskan Indians live here – the Kutchin, Han, Tuchone, Inland Tlingit, Kasha and the Tagish. The Inuit have lived along the Yukon's north coast for most of the last 5,000 years. The territory has the second-highest rate of common-law unions in Canada. In 1991, almost 20% of families in the Yukon were common-law – twice the national average.

Newfoundland

- Population, 1991: 568,474
- Population by mother tongue, 1986: English, 98.8%; French, 0.5%; Other, 0.8%
- Proportion urban, 1986: 58.9%
- Area (square kilometres): 405,720

"The Rock" has Canada's highest share of English-speakers – almost all of the population has English as a mother tongue. This is partly due, no doubt, to Newfoundland's harsh climate and terrain, high unemployment and struggling economy – all have discouraged immigrants from settling in the province. Not surprisingly, Newfoundland has the lowest rate of bilingualism in the country – only 2.6% spoke both English and French in 1986. Canada's most easterly province also has the highest rate of religious affiliation in the country – 1981, only 1% of the population had no religious ties.

Prince Edward Island

- Population, 1991: 129,765
- Population by mother tongue, 1986: English, 94.1%; French, 4.7%; Other, 1.2%
- Proportion urban, 1986: 38.1%
- Area (square kilometres): 5,660

Often called "Spud Island" after its major crop, potatoes, Prince Edward Island is the least urbanized part of Canada – almost two-thirds of the population lived outside urban areas in 1986. P.E.I.'s small size has made it the most densely populated province, with 22.4 persons per square kilometre. As in Newfoundland, living common-law is relatively uncommon in P.E.I.; in 1991 only 6.0% of families were common-law.

Nova Scotia

- Population, 1991: 899,942
- Population by mother tongue, 1986: English, 93.8%; French, 4.1%; Other, 2.1%
- Proportion urban, 1986: 54%
- Area (square kilometres): 52,841

Like the rest of Atlantic Canada, Nova Scotia has relatively few one-person households. Few immigrants choose Nova Scotia, but the province has one of the largest concentrations of blacks in Canada. This is because hundreds of blacks came here in the wake of the American revolution, and several thousand more followed after the War of 1812 between Britain and the United States. The province's fertility rate is below the national average.

New Brunswick

- Population, 1991: 723,900
- Population by mother tongue, 1986: English, 65.3%; French, 33.5%; Other, 1.3%
- Proportion urban, 1986: 49.4%
- Area (square kilometres): 71,769

New Brunswick is the second-most bilingual province after Quebec – more than 29% of the population spoke both English and French in 1986. The province also has a large French minority – more than 33% of New Brunswickers had French as their mother tongue in 1986. As with the rest of the Atlantic region, few immigrants come to New Brunswick. The province's divorce and fertility rates are below the national average.

Quebec

- Population, 1991: 6,895,963
- Population by mother tongue, 1986: English, 10.4%; French, 82.8%; Other, 6.8%
- Proportion urban, 1986: 77.9%
- Area (square kilometres): 1,375,655

Quebec is the only province with a French-speaking majority – more than 80%. Quebec is also the most religiously uniform part of Canada; in 1981, more than 88% of Quebecers had ties to the Roman Catholic Church. And no other part of Canada can match Quebec for bilingualism – in 1986, 34.5% of the population spoke English and French. The share of families that are common-law (16.3%) is the third-highest in the country. For many years Quebec had the lowest fertility rates in the country, but in 1989, Newfoundland's rate was lower.

Ontario

- Population, 1991: 10,084,885
- Population by mother tongue, 1986: English, 78%; French, 5.3%; Other, 16.7%
- Proportion urban, 1986: 82.6%
- Area (square kilometres): 916,735

Canada's most populous province is the intended destination of more than half of the country's immigrants. It also takes in more migrants from other parts of Canada than any other province. Together, these trends should ensure strong population growth. The Toronto region alone is expected to top 5 million before the turn of the century. Ontario is tied with Saskatchewan for the lowest share of male-led one-parent families (2.1%). Ontario is the most urbanized part of the country.

Manitoba

- Population, 1991: 1,091,942
- Population by mother tongue, 1986: English, 73.4%; French, 4.9%; Other, 21.8%
- Proportion urban, 1986: 72.1%
- Area (square kilometres): 547,704

Manitoba's share of seniors is almost twice the national average;

those aged 65 and older made up 13.4% of the province's population in 1991. Manitoba has a sizeable French community – almost 5% of Manitobans had French as a mother tongue in 1986. It is also the fourth most bilingual province – almost 9% of Manitobans spoke English and French in 1986. The province's divorce rate is lower than the national average, but its fertility rate is higher.

Saskatchewan

- Population, 1991: 988,928
- Population by mother tongue, 1986: English, 81.9%; French, 2.3%; Other, 15.7%
- Proportion urban, 1986: 61.4%
- Area (square kilometres): 570,113

Saskatchewan is often associated with endless wheat fields and farmsteads. Yet despite its reliance on grain farming, the province is highly urbanized – a larger share of the population lived in urban areas in 1986 than in Newfoundland, Nova Scotia, New Brunswick, the Northwest Territories or Prince Edward Island. Saskatchewan has Canada's ''oldest'' population; in 1991, 14.1% were aged 65 and older. The ''greying'' of Saskatchewan is due in part to an exodus of young people. In 1990, the province had a net population loss of more than 15,000, by far the largest loss in Canada. This drain made Saskatchewan's population drop below 1,000,000 for the first time since 1984.

Alberta

- Population, 1991: 2,545,553
- Population by mother tongue, 1986: English, 82.3%; French, 2.4%; Other, 15.3%
- Proportion urban, 1986: 79.4%
- Area (square kilometres): 638,233

Alberta is the fourth most popular destination for immigrants to Canada, attracting almost 8% of the total in 1991. Alberta is also a big draw for migrants from other parts of Canada: in 1990, more than 77,000 moved to Alberta. In that same year, Alberta and British Columbia were the only provinces that had more people moving in than out. Alberta is Canada's second-most urbanized province.

British Columbia

- Population, 1991: 3,282,061
- Population by mother tongue, 1986: English, 82.1%; French, 1.6%; Other, 16.3%
- Proportion urban, 1986: 79.3%
- Area (square kilometres): 892,677

The mild winters and warm summers of the West Coast have earned B.C. the nicknames ''Lotusland'' and ''British California''. The climate is a magnet for retired Canadians. This helps explain why B.C.'s 65-and-older population is among the fastest-growing in Canada. B.C.'s ethnic Chinese community numbers more than 100,000; most live in Vancouver, which has the second-largest Chinese community in North America. British Columbia has the second-highest divorce rate after Alberta, and about one in five residents has no religious affiliation – the highest share in Canada.

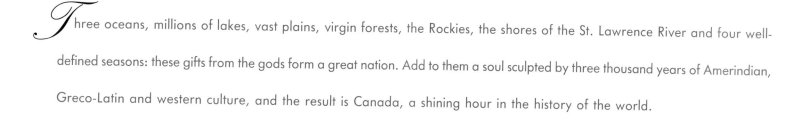

Three oceans, millions of lakes, vast plains, virgin forests, the Rockies, the shores of the St. Lawrence River and four well-defined seasons: these gifts from the gods form a great nation. Add to them a soul sculpted by three thousand years of Amerindian, Greco-Latin and western culture, and the result is Canada, a shining hour in the history of the world.

Antonine Maillet, born in Bouctouche, New Brunswick. Contemporary Acadian novelist, recipient of the Prix Goncourt (France), Companion of the Order of Canada.

Canada's society is people – our values, customs and beliefs as individuals, the ways we arrange ourselves in groups, the ways we make decisions, the values we hold in common. Indeed, Canada's values are mirrored in the way we have structured our society.

We have a system of government adapted from the world's great democracies. Among its features are universal health care, social security from cradle to grave and highly accessible education. Canada also has an advanced communications system that connects us with one another and the world.

This chapter presents information on this infrastructure from both contemporary and historic perspectives.

The Government and Legal System

The Constitution   The Canadian Constitution is more than a beautifully decorated proclamation sealed in a climate-controlled vault at the National Archives. It is a continuing process – some might say a persisting argument – about Canadian society's basic structure and institutions.

Canada is a constitutional monarchy, a federal state and a parliamentary democracy, with two systems of law and two official languages, English and French. Legislative power is divided between Parliament and 10 provincial legislatures.

Yet in Canada, the tension of joining federal and parliamentary systems – and two official languages – has never been fully resolved. Although a strong and vigorous hybrid system has adapted and flourished since 1867, debate is never far away. Indeed, Canada's Constitution Act has been amended more than 20 times since it was first passed into law in 1867. By ''patriating'' its Constitution in 1982, Canada finally gained the right to amend it without having to address the British Parliament. While the federal government and nine provinces signed the constitutional accord that made this possible, Quebec declined.

In the late 1980s, the debate began again, with provincial and federal first ministers suggesting new provincial powers coupled with recognition of Quebec as a distinct society in the Meech Lake Accord. All provincial legislatures were to approve the accord before it could be added to the Constitution, but two legislatures did not and the accord died.

As the debate has continued, other groups have also demanded constitutional changes. In 1991, to deal with the aspirations of Quebec and of Canada's aboriginal peoples, the federal government appointed cabinet minister Joe Clark, a former prime minister, to seek the opinions of Canadians on possible solutions.

On February 28, 1992, the *Report of the Special Joint Committee on a Renewed Canada* – known as the ''Beaudoin-Dobbie Report'' – was released. It called for recognition of Quebec as a distinct society with veto powers over changes to the parliamentary system. It suggested enlarging provincial powers in certain areas. It recommended recognizing the inherent right of aboriginal peoples to self-government. It advised changing the Senate, notably to make it an elected body. It called for a federal law requiring a national referendum to confirm or help shape constitutional change, and a ''social covenant'' committing government to medicare, social services, quality education, collective bargaining and a clean environment. Lastly, it called for a ''Canada clause'' that would outline the characteristics of the country.

As *Canada: A Portrait* went to press, the constitutional debate was continuing. In 1943, just before he died, John W. Dafoe, 78, a veteran political commentator and editorial writer for the *Winnipeg Free Press*, told a friend, ''I wish I could stick around a while to see how things turn out.'' He might easily be saying the same thing today.

Whatever the outcome, the Canadian Constitution nonetheless sets up basic structures through which Canadians formally deal with each other. It frames the country's system of law and justice. It defines federal and provincial governments, their powers and how they are elected. It also sets out citizens' basic rights and liberties.

Federal power is divided between the government's legislative, executive and judicial branches. Elected representatives in the legislature adopt laws and vote on taxes and other money-related matters. The executive proposes legislation, presents budgets to the legislature and implements laws. The judiciary is the final interpreter of the laws.

''Let us never forget that, because a Constitution is what it is, pervading and shaping the lives of every human being in the community, changing it by formal amendment is an immensely serious business. It is not like getting a new hair-do, or growing a beard, or buying a new piece of furniture or new clothes, or putting in a new bathroom. It is more like marriage: 'Not by any to be enterprised, nor taken in hand, unadvisedly, lightly, or wantonly . . . but reverently, discreetly, advisedly, soberly and in the fear of God.' What we are dealing with in constitutional change is not paper or things. It is human lives.''

Senator Eugene Forsey, Canadian constitutional expert. ''Our Present Discontents''. 1974.

Canadians have lived under a monarchy since the first French regime in the 1600s. Today, Canada's Queen and head of state, Her Majesty Queen Elizabeth II, lives in Great Britain. She delegates her duties – largely ceremonial – to her representative in Canada, the Governor General.

The cabinet, headed by the prime minister, holds the government's actual authority. At present about 40 government ministers compose cabinet. The prime minister, who holds extensive powers himself, usually chooses cabinet ministers from among the governing party's elected members of Parliament, although he may also name senators to cabinet.

Strictly speaking, the prime minister and cabinet advise the Queen. Practically speaking, though, cabinet holds the actual power, and the Governor General usually acts on cabinet's advice.

Cabinet, which develops government policy, is responsible to Parliament's House of Commons. The Government of Canada, headed by cabinet, performs its duties through federal departments, special boards and commissions, and Crown corporations.

Provincial governments have a parallel structure to that of the federal government. Lieutenant governors represent the Queen in the provinces, each of which has a premier and a cabinet, who are also responsible for provincial departments, commissions and Crown corporations.

The prime minister and the premiers, in principle, usually lead the political party that gained the largest number of seats in the legislature in the most recent election. There are exceptions. For instance, the Governor General or a lieutenant governor may ask the leader of a party with fewer seats to form a government if the previous government resigns.

The Charter of Rights and Freedoms   To protect rights and freedoms, the architects of Canada's Confederation followed Britain's example. In 1867 they included safeguards established by the courts, and by great documents such as the British Magna Carta, in Canada's Constitution.

In 1982, the Charter of Rights and Freedoms was written into the Constitution Act to protect basic human rights. These rights include: freedom of association and assembly; freedom of thought, conscience and religion; freedom of the press; the right to vote in federal and provincial elections; rights to free movement; rights to residence; language rights; equality rights; and legal guarantees such as the right to consult a lawyer, the right to a fair trial, the right to be presumed innocent until proven guilty, and the right to be protected against unreasonable searches, arbitrary imprisonment and cruel punishments. Special provisions also protect native rights.

The Federal Government   Canada's system of government borrows ideas from Britain and the United States.

The Constitution defines a federal system of government. This means that law-making authority is divided between the Parliament of Canada and the provincial legislatures. At the federal

level, legislative power is divided between two houses of government: the Senate and the House of Commons.

Federal responsibilities include national defence; trade other than local; shipping; the federal public service; the banking and monetary system; criminal law; and fisheries. Parliament also holds residual powers over all areas not mentioned or not discovered when the first Constitution was written – for instance, aeronautics, radio, nuclear energy, and offshore mineral rights.

Provincial legislatures are responsible for education, property and civil rights, the administration of justice, the hospital system, natural resources within their borders, social security, health and municipal institutions.

There are also areas where the two levels of government share jurisdiction, for example, housing, policing and prisons.

The Yukon and the Northwest Territories are special cases, and differ from provinces. Legislative assemblies govern the territories, and commissioners have duties similar to those of lieutenant governors, but they report to the minister of Indian and Northern Affairs, who has jurisdiction over renewable and non-renewable natural resources.

Municipal governments created by the provinces look after local matters such as police and fire protection, local courts and jails, sanitation, snow removal, road maintenance and public education.

The House of Commons Canadian Senator Eugene Forsey summed up the idea behind Canada's Parliament this way:

"Parliamentary government is not just a matter of counting heads instead of breaking them. It is also a matter of using them. It is government by discussion, not just by majority. Parliament is not just a voting place. It is also, pre-eminently, essentially, a talking place, a *parlement*."

Canada adopted the parliamentary system from Great Britain. In Canada, the House of Commons, also called the lower house, has 295 members. Canada is currently divided into 295 electoral districts, based on the principle of representation by population. These districts are revised after each national 10-year census. In each district, Canadian citizens aged 18 and older elect a single member, in one round of voting, although Nova Scotia has had double ridings in the past.

To remain in power, the government must have the confidence of a majority of members in the House of Commons. If defeated in a vote of nonconfidence in the House, the government must resign or ask the Governor General to dissolve Parliament.

The Senate Sir James Lougheed, Conservative Senate leader from 1906 to 1921, is said to have called Canada's Senate "a bulwark against the clamour and caprice of the mob." Canada's first prime minister, Sir John A. MacDonald, called it "the sober second thought in legislation."

The Senate, also known as the upper house, reviews bills passed by the House of Commons. Patterned after the British House of Lords, its 104 members are appointed, and represent the country's regions: Ontario, Quebec, the West, and the Maritimes

Federal Government Expenditure

Year	
1990	
1985	
1980	
1975	
1970	
1965	
1960	

0   5   10   15   20   25
(% of GDP)

Source: Statistics Canada

each has 24 members. In addition, Newfoundland has six members, and the Yukon and the Northwest Territories each has one member.

The Senate has been a focus of the recent constitutional debate, with many Canadians calling for reforms that would give regions outside Quebec and Ontario more seats, and require members to be elected.

While the Senate has legislative powers similar to those of the House of Commons, it cannot hold a vote of nonconfidence, initiate public spending bills, or veto bills to amend the Constitution, although it may suspend these bills for 180 days.

Bills receive three readings in each house, then receive royal assent – the final approval – in the Senate.

In the provinces, single-house legislatures have become the rule. Upper chambers, where they existed, have been abolished.

The Legal System   Canada's legal system draws from two traditions. Principles of common law used in most Canadian provinces were first formed in medieval England. Principles of Quebec's *le droit civil* go back through France to the ancient Roman Empire.

Both traditions are based on the rule of law: all citizens – and the government – are subject to, and equal before, the law. Canadians have built on these traditions to meet their own needs, changing old laws and writing new ones. As well, courts interpret and enforce the law to reflect changing values and circumstances.

Provincial governments have authority to make laws about education, property rights, administration of justice, municipalities and other matters of a local or private nature. In addition, the provinces may create local or municipal governments that can then make bylaws dealing with matters such as parking or local building standards.

The federal government deals with areas affecting all of Canada – for instance trade and commerce, national defence, immigration and criminal law.

Within these limits, Parliament or provincial or territorial legislatures can make or change laws by enacting written statutes. Such statute laws automatically take the place of any unwritten common law precedents that deal with the same subject, but they may be challenged and overturned in the courts.

Any parliamentary or legislative member may propose a new law. Usually, though, the government in power puts forward most new laws. A proposed law must be presented to the entire Parliament or legislative assembly for study and debate. Only if a proposed law is approved by a majority vote of members, does it become a statute law, and then only after royal assent and proclamation.

Common Law and the Civil Code   Not all Canadian laws are statute laws. Common law traditions also support many unwritten legal principles. This is especially true of civil law, which deals with private matters between individuals, such as property ownership, family obligations and business deals.

Civil law in nine of Canada's 10 provinces is based on common

1990 Criminal Code Charges

• Police reported more than 2.6 million Criminal Code offences in 1990. The crime rate of 9,907 offences per 100,000 population was an increase of 7% over 1989.

Between 1989 and 1990:

• Narcotic and drug offences fell 12%.
• Violent crime increased 7%. Violent crime in Canada has increased more than 50% over the last 10 years.
• Property crime increased 7%. In this category, vehicle thefts increased 12% to a record high of 113,639; credit card frauds increased 29%; business break-ins rose 12%; and home break-ins rose 6%.
• In 1990 there were 656 murders in a population of 26 million, the number virtually unchanged from 1989.
• Some 83% of all persons charged under the Criminal Code were males.

law, a system built on precedent: whenever a judge makes a legal decision, this decision becomes a precedent – a rule that will guide other judges who consider similar cases later. Many of Canada's laws are based on such precedents as well as customary practices, developed over the years.

Quebec's civil law, called *le droit civil*, is based on a written code, called "*le Code civil*," which is a thorough list of rules for different kinds of cases. When a judge considers a case under *le droit civil*, he or she first checks this written code for guidance, then looks for precedents set by earlier decisions.

Although the approaches of common law and *le droit civil* differ, their results often do not. In similar cases, the two systems usually produce similar results.

The Courts   Courts interpret and apply Canadian laws. Parliament has established several courts, and each province has its own courts, which deal with both federal and provincial laws.

The Supreme Court of Canada is the highest court in the country, set up in 1949 to replace appeals to Britain's Privy Council. It is established by federal statute and judges are appointed by the prime minister. This court hears appeals from provincial superior courts, and its decision is always final.

The federal Parliament has also established the Federal Court, which deals with claims made against the government, and matters like patents, copyrights and maritime law.

The Tax Court, another federally established court, rules on tax matters.

In addition to these courts, Canada has a number of federal boards and tribunals that deal with administrative rules and regulations in areas such as broadcasting licences, safety standards and labour relations.

Provinces divide their court systems into two or three levels. At the first level are provincial courts, which deal with most criminal offences, and small claims courts, which deal with private disputes involving small sums of money. Judges for these courts, which may also include specialized youth and family courts, are appointed by provincial governments.

District or county courts are at the next level. These handle some criminal cases, appeals from lower courts and private disputes involving larger sums of money. The federal government appoints judges at this level. Most of the provinces have joined their district or county courts with their superior courts.

A superior court, which deals with the most serious cases, stands at the highest level in each province. The federal government appoints the judges. A division of this court (or a separate Court of Appeal) also hears appeals from all the lower courts.

Legal Advice   Lawyers are regulated by provincial law societies that set standards for joining the society and for practicing law in each province.

All provinces have publicly funded legal programs that give persons of limited financial means free or low-cost legal advice. Rules for these programs differ in each province, but they all make proper legal representation available to everyone who needs it, whatever their income.

Law Enforcement   Canada's image abroad is of red-coated Mounties in wide Stetson hats astride horses. But today's Mountie is more likely to sit at a computer.

The Royal Canadian Mounted Police (RCMP), a technologically sophisticated national police force with 13,000 peace officers and 7,000 civilian employees, enforces many federal laws, particularly criminal and narcotics laws. It also represents Canada internationally as a member of the International Criminal Police Organization (INTERPOL).

The RCMP is the only police force in the Yukon and the Northwest Territories. Eight provinces also pay the RCMP to police within their borders.

The RCMP has crime-detection laboratories across Canada, a computerized police information centre, the Canadian Police College in Ottawa and a training academy in Regina. The college offers advanced courses to members of other police forces in Canada and around the world.

Municipal police forces provide general police services in local areas. Where there is no municipal force, a federal or provincial police force performs these duties.

Communications

Never have Marshall McLuhan's words been more apt: ''We live today in the Age of Information and of Communication

because electric media instantly and constantly create a total field of interacting events in which all [people] participate.'' Communications technology is reshaping our lives. At any downtown intersection in Canada, you may see people talking on cellular telephones as they drive, cycle or walk – or perhaps a person in a parked car sending a document through a briefcase fax machine.

Information industries help drive Canada's economy, and some experts suggest they employ as much as half the labour force. Some experts say that this developing ''information age'' is as significant as Canada's earlier shift from an agricultural to an industrial society.

Canada's information sector is fed by the electronic equivalent of a central nervous system, a national web linking machines that create, store and exchange information. These machines range in power and complexity from home and car telephones to automatic bank tellers, from personal computers and facsimile machines to giant mainframe and super computers that run stock exchanges, support government social services, or forecast weather.

Personal computers can ''talk'' by telephone to other computers. Hundreds of computerized electronic ''bulletin boards'' let individuals post and collect messages. Large national networks work in a similar way, forming an information market of electronic news services, stock market updates, and a host of other information and entertainment services.

Fibre Optics A coast-to-coast fibre-optic system, which can move huge amounts of high quality voice or computer information using light rather than conventional electronic signals, is close to complete in Canada. A single traditional copper telephone wire can carry no more than 24 separate conversations at one time. A single fibre-optic cable of about the same size can carry 10,000, or more than 400 times as many calls.
It's as if, by replacing a water hose with a new one that looks the same, you could suddenly pour more than 400 separate streams of water, all as big and fast as the first – and each a different colour.

Computer Literacy
Canada is a computer literate nation. Statistics Canada found that in 1989, some 9.6 million Canadian adults – close to half the adult population aged 15 years and older – knew how to use a computer, and about 4 million, or 19%, had a personal computer at home. Some 4.2 million Canadians, or about a third of all people who were employed at the time, used personal computers at work.
The ability to use a computer was highest among Alberta, British Columbia and Ontario residents, and among people younger than 25.

Good communication has always been crucial to Canadian society, pulling together a population scattered over vast distances, and physically isolated by difficult climate and terrain. Hence Canadians have often been leaders in developing and applying new communications technologies. These have included telegraph, telephone and telex systems; radio; television; land-based microwave transmitters; fibre optics; digital communication; and communications satellites that bounce broadcast signals and telephone calls to every corner of the country. Linked with other nations' systems, Canada's telecommunications contribute to globalization, creating an electronic world transcending national borders.

Many countries have unified state-controlled post, telephone and telegraph systems. Because of its large area and diverse needs, Canada has a telecommunications industry with more dispersed ownership. Federal or provincial governments run some parts, private businesses run others, and government and business work as partners in the rest.

Telecommunications More than 98% of Canadian households have telephones – 68% have two or more – and that makes us a world leader. Canadians also have a history of talking on telephones more than any other people. In 1990, we dialed 3.1 billion long-distance toll calls and an uncounted number of local calls. In 1990, about 62 telephone systems provided public telephone service, earning operating revenues of $13.3 billion.

National telecommunications carriers include Telecom Canada, a group of phone companies that transmit long-distance voice and data messages; Telesat Canada, the national satellite carrier; Unitel, evolved from 19th century railroad telegraph companies into a business and data communications service; television cable companies; and Teleglobe Canada, which handles overseas links.

Less Government Private ownership has been increasing in Canadian communications. Private business has bought shares of government-owned Crown corporations such as Teleglobe Canada and Unitel, and in early 1992 the federal government placed its shares of Telesat on sale.

This matches other industrialized countries. Worldwide, public telecommunications monopolies are being sold to the private sector, although these services retain public service obligations and are strictly regulated.

The trend toward business-style operations has reached conventional mail service. The 10 billion parcels and messages Canada Post delivers each year now include electronic mail, courier, and fast delivery services, all of which compete with private services. This former government department became a Crown corporation in 1981, and began hiring private contractors to handle parts of its operations.

Broadcasting In early 1991, there were some 5,456 commercial radio and television outlets in operation, including transmitters, relay transmitters, and cable and pay TV services.

Responsibility for Canada's broadcasting policies rests with the federal department of communications (Communications Canada) and the Canadian Radio-television and Telecommunications Commission (CRTC) which regulates broadcasting.

In 1990-91 the Canadian Broadcasting Corporation (CBC) had an annual budget of $1.4 billion, of which $985 million came from parliamentary appropriations. It ran television, mono radio, and stereo radio networks, each in English and French. The CBC also operates Newsworld – an all-news cable channel that receives no public funding – and broadcasts worldwide in seven languages on the Radio Canada International shortwave radio service. The latter is funded by External Affairs and International Trade Canada.

In addition, a vast network of private radio and TV broadcasters, with total operating revenues of roughly $2 billion in 1989, deliver programs to local and national markets.

In 1990, some 1,747 cable television systems operating in Canada serviced 7 million subscribers. A further 325 were licensed but not yet operating. Altogether they reported $1.6 billion in revenues.

Basic cable service is only part of the picture. Specialty channels show news, sports, youth programming, weather information and music videos. Pay TV channels play movies or news for extra cost, and "pay per view" channels sell viewers movies and special events, by the program.

The Information Society   Processing information of all types may well be at the heart of Canada's economy in the future.

Tuned In From phone-in television shows in which viewers talk to favourite rock groups live, to constitutional conferences across Canada, to pointed questions on national issues in the House of Commons, to a tense stand-off between natives and the armed forces at Oka, electronic communications plug Canadians into what's happening, anywhere, fast. In 1991, Statistics Canada found that some 99% of Canadian households owned at least one radio (80% had two or more), 97% had at least one colour television, and 69% owned a videocassette recorder. In 1989, the last year for which Statistics Canada published figures, the average Canadian watched 23 hours of television each week – the least in the past decade, but only by one hour.

It will be a changed world. Economist Dian Cohen puts it this way: "I would try to get all Canadians to understand that in an information economy they have to think upside down. Money is kept in investments, where it earns interest. Information that is hoarded carries a negative interest rate: the longer you hoard it without acting on it, the less it's worth."

Telecommunications and computer technologies have converged to create a new field – information technology. Canadians are increasingly finding ways to create, distribute and use information to provide the jobs, wealth and social progress that traditionally came from exploiting raw materials and physical labour. The information sector of Canada's economy has grown faster than any other during the past 40 years. Communications Canada says information workers accounted for as much as 45% of total employment in the country in 1986.

What's Coming Communications are Canada's leading high technology area. More than one-quarter of the country's industrial research and development involves communications, and Canadian communications companies are world famous. New products are developed by business, government, universities, or some combination of these in partnership.

Canadian communications researchers, like others in the world, are making less do more. Equipment has been shrunk to a microscopic scale but can handle more amounts and types of information. More and more channels are loaded into the crowded electronic "space" of radio bands and land circuits.

Technology is also creating new kinds of communications networks and new uses for old ones. Communications satellites, which Canada pioneered and continues to develop, are expanding the capabilities of telephone, television and data communications nets.

In 1994, a Telesat subsidiary will launch the world's first dedicated domestic mobile communications satellite. A portable satellite earth station that looks like an ordinary briefcase already exists, and will bounce microwave radio signals off the satellite to any telephone exchange in the country, even from isolated arctic islands or mountain tops. Researchers are developing even smaller earth stations.

Canada is digitizing its communications network faster than any other country. This means it is coding messages in the efficient language of computers rather than in older-style electrical waves, known as "analogue communication". In the late 1980s, more than 70% of electronic messages moved digitally between Canadian cities, some on copper coaxial cable, some on fibre-optic cable. As a result, telephone conversations sound clearer, and there is less chance of losing information in data messages.

Data messages can already be transmitted at astonishing speeds. The best of today's commonly available commercial modems will transmit a 100-page single-spaced document in about 40 seconds under ideal conditions. One data interface based on fibre optics is theoretically capable of sending the same document in .0001 second – far faster than any personal computer can handle.

Canadian research also focuses on Integrated Services Digital Network (ISDN) standards. Equipment designed using this set of international standards would result in powerful new capabilities, revolutionizing telecommunications around the world. With ISDN, a person using a telephone could send a hand-drawn diagram and a computer screen full of data, on the same telephone line, in the middle of a conversation. Telecommunications carriers in Canada, Japan, the United States, Germany and France are now holding ISDN trials and offering limited service. But because it has already digitized many of its electronic communications, Canada will be able to use ISDN capabilities faster than most other countries.

In Canada, different laws regulate different types of communication. However, as technologies converge, once-distinct boundaries will blur. Full fibre-optic ISDN service, for example, would let a single line feed a cable television, a remote burglar alarm, a computer terminal and a telephone simultaneously.

Telephone, cable television, telecommunications data, or satellite broadcasting companies, or some new combination, theoretically would be capable of supplying this kind of ''super service.'' However, the possibility of overlapping services poses new questions for the industry and for government regulators.

After passing a new broadcast act in 1991, the government in early 1992 began debate on a new telecommunications bill to deal with these issues and others brought on by changing communications technology.

E   d   u   c   a   t   i   o   n

In 1905, Canadian educator Sir William Osler wrote that ''The value of a really great student to the country is equal to half a dozen grain elevators or a new transcontinental railway.'' Time has made his statement prophesy, and Canadians are enrolling in universities and colleges in unprecedented numbers. Experts predict that two out of every three jobs created in Canada in the next decade will need more than 12 years of schooling – and two out of five will need 16 years or more.

The trend has already started. In the 1990-91 recession, overall employment fell slightly. The number of blue-collar jobs plunged, but the number of white-collar jobs – those for university-educated people – actually increased.

Canadians today understand that education is crucial, both for themselves and for society. Canada spent more of its Gross Domestic Product (GDP) (GDP is a measure of the value of all goods and services produced in the economy) on education than any other G-7 nation between 1980 and 1988 – about 7% – according to the United Nations Educational, Scientific and Cultural Organization (UNESCO). (The G-7 comprises the seven largest western industrialized economies, those of the United States, Japan, Germany, France, Italy, the United Kingdom and Canada). Of this, about 2% of GDP went to higher education. Canadian spending on all types of education totalled an estimated $50.6 billion in 1991-92.

The Costs of Education

1990 - 91
1990

1985 - 86
1985

1980 - 81
1980

1975 - 76
1975

1970 - 71
1970

-0   5   10   15   20   25
(% change from previous year)

■ Government education expenditures
(fiscal year)

■ Consumer Price Index
(calendar year)

Source: Statistics Canada

Only social welfare programs – another part of Canada's social infrastructure – take a bigger share of GDP.

Literacy and Learning   The Organization for Economic Co-operation and Development (OECD) says that improving literacy would make Canada – and probably all other industrialized countries – more productive and competitive.

A 1989 Statistics Canada survey of literacy found a strong relationship between everyday reading skills and high school graduation. And generally, Canadians with university education had higher levels of literacy than high school grads. Gender was not a factor among Canadian-born men and women, but age was – younger people had better everyday reading skills. Higher income was also linked with better reading skills.

In the survey, Statistics Canada found that 62% of Canadian adults can handle most everyday reading tasks in at least one of Canada's two official languages. They also have the skills to acquire further knowledge using printed material, going beyond what they already know.

Another 22% can do simple reading tasks as long as the subject is familiar, and laid out clearly. But the reading skills of 16% of all adult Canadians – about 2.9 million people – are too limited to deal with most everyday written material. Of those, 2% reported having no reading skills at all in English or French. And compared to their male counterparts and the Canadian-born population, women immigrants to Canada generally have more difficulty reading.

Elementary and Secondary Schools   Each province operates its own public education system, and provincial and municipal governments pay most education costs. This means education systems differ across the country.

However, public education is generally divided into elementary, junior high school, and high school grades. Levels within elementary-secondary schools vary by province. Elementary covers the first six grades in most jurisdictions; in others, Grades 7 and 8 are also considered elementary. Consequently, inter-provincial variations also exist at secondary (high) schools. These schools include five or six grades, and may be further subdivided into junior high, senior high and junior-senior high schools. By law, children must attend school between the ages of 6 and 15 or 16, or must be schooled at home under the supervision of local authorities.

Alternatives   Some alternative elementary and secondary schools operate outside the public system. Such private or independent schools may tailor programs to religious, linguistic, or social groups or to students with special needs.

Newfoundland, Quebec, Ontario, Saskatchewan, Alberta and the Northwest Territories provide for public school systems based on religion.

Postsecondary Education   Full-time university enrollments in Canada rose sharply in the late 1960s and early 1970s, fueled by post-Second World War baby boomers. Educators thought this surge was temporary, and that enrollments would drop again in the wake of lower birth rates after the baby boom.

The proportion of university-age Canadians has indeed fallen, but full-time student enrollment is still increasing. A growing proportion of Canadians now enter university. Between 1980 and 1988, full-time enrollment at Canada's universities rose 30%, from 382,600 to close to half a million. If current trends continue, enrollments will increase until at least the year 2000.

University enrollment also indicates a move toward sexual equality in Canadian society. Between 1980 and 1988, undergraduate enrollment rates for women rose 44%, compared with 18% for men. In 1989, full-time female university students slightly outnumbered males for the first time ever.

The number of graduate students has also increased. Between 1980 and 1988, full-time graduate enrollment rose 34%.

Funding   In 1992 the federal Unity Committee proposed that access to adequate education be part of a ''social covenant'' written into the Canadian Constitution. Indeed, many Canadians see education, along with social benefits like pensions and medicare, as a basic part of society's infrastructure.

Canadians support their universities and colleges mostly through taxes and have consistently spent about 2% of the GDP on universities. But enrollment has grown more quickly than the GDP during the past few years, which means universities have less to spend on each student.

This reversed a trend started in the 1960s, when funding per student rose 66% in real terms. During the 1970s it also rose, but more slowly, at 13.2%. In the 1980s it fell 6%.

The people who run Canadian universities say they need to counter declining funding by cutting academic budgets. This means capping enrollments, stiffening admission standards, raising tuition fees, cutting staff or all of these.

A concern in the coming decade may be a shortage of teaching faculty. If present trends continue, the demand for university instructors will increase faster than the supply of doctoral graduates in all disciplines until at least the year 2000.

Canada's academic labour market is part of a wider national and international labour market. The trend everywhere is toward higher education. As business and U.S. universities and colleges offer higher salaries to doctoral and masters graduates, Canadian universities may find it harder to hire and keep academic staff.

Canadian universities carry out about 25% of the country's research and development (R&D). Because Canada also spends a smaller proportion of its GDP on R&D than other developed nations, staff shortages and tight money at universities could affect the country's R&D efforts.

Health and Social Security

Health and Behaviour   Bob Edwards, editor of a scrappy little Canadian frontier newspaper, the *Calgary Eye Opener*, observed in the early 1900s that ''When one is driven to drink, he usually has to walk back.'' These days, fewer Canadians take the trip – rough-edged frontier attitudes have moderated. Drinking, along with smoking and drug use, have declined. Exercise and eating habits have improved, part of a movement toward healthier lifestyles.

For instance, more of us are walking, gardening, swimming, cycling or dancing. A Statistics Canada survey found the number of Canadian adults who could be labelled ''very active,'' based on the amount of energy they spent on leisure pursuits, rose from 27% in 1985 to 32% in 1991. Generally, the number of good health practices Canadians follow – the healthiness of their lifestyles – increases with age and education.

The amount of alcohol we drink has been falling, according to a number of surveys, for more than 10 years. Statistics Canada found that in 1978, 65% of adults were ''current drinkers'' – that is, they drank alcohol at least once a month. By 1991, that had fallen to 55%. For both sexes, drinking peaks at ages 20 to 24, then falls with age. Relatively few Canadians drink heavily. In 1991, 10% of current drinkers had 14 or more drinks a week. Heavy drinking was more common among men (15% of current drinkers) than among women (4% of current drinkers), a difference that held for all ages.

Drinking preferences are shifting, too. From 1982 to 1986, spirits sales fell 20% and beer sales fell 4%, while wine sales jumped 9%.

Alcohol causes no problems for most Canadians. But studies link from 4,000 to 5,000 deaths each year to unsafe drinking.

Alcohol-related problems are a major cause of early death among youth, and alcohol abuse contributes to many illnesses. The total cost of alcohol abuse is estimated at $5 billion a year in Canada.

Smoking, the leading preventable cause of illness in Canada, accounts for 38,000 deaths each year. However, Statistics Canada found in 1991 that 26% of adults smoked daily, down from 41% in 1966. While the rate among men dropped to 26% in 1991 from 54% in 1966, the rate among women dropped only slightly – to 26% from 28%. And a Health and Welfare Canada study shows that lately, smokers tend to light up fewer cigarettes per day.

Canada has taken firm steps to counter the dangers of smoking. Cigarette companies must print warnings about the health hazards of smoking in large letters on each pack they sell. Federal laws also restrict tobacco advertising and sales, and since 1989 have clamped down on smoking in government work places, in public places and on most intercity buses and airplanes.

As well, by 1990 about 150 towns and cities had bylaws to restrict tobacco use in public. Experts say this number could double by 1992.

Changing and Aging Canada's population is aging, and Canadian health and social security systems – already the most costly part of society's infrastructure – will bear the brunt.

Worldwide, on average, those aged over 75 use up to 10 times as much health care as those aged between 20 and 50. Canada may be no different. And pension funds may be drained as never before, because more people may start drawing from them at the same time as the pool of working-age contributors begins to dry up. Already, social security spending consumes the largest portion of the federal budget – about 38% in 1992-93. The number of seniors drawing Canada Pension Plan (CPP) benefits is expected to increase by 40% between 1991 and the year 2000.

Social security may also be affected by globalization – the trend toward viewing the world as a single, very large community with increasingly transparent borders. Governments are losing some of the financial levers they once used to manage national programs and economies. International money market investors move assets to the country that offers the best combination of security and investment return; international trade agreements like GATT restrict a country's ability to protect its own industries; and large multinational businesses make decisions that on occasion run counter to national interests.

As these conditions accelerate, Canadians may see more outside influences on their society's infrastructure.

Canada already has arrangements with other countries – to control hazardous substances, to counter illegal drug traffic, and to identify communicable diseases. It also has made some reciprocal social security arrangements.

Some experts say that as globalization increases, Canada may find itself pressured, for instance, to sign new worldwide social security agreements that would help immigrants and emigrants qualify for pensions based on the periods they live and work in each country.

Health Care Canadians generally feel good about their personal health: a 1990 Statistics Canada survey found that 26% rated their health excellent, 36% thought it was very good, and 26% rated it good.

Compared with people of most other countries, Canadians live longer and have more healthy, productive years. In the past 20 years, for instance, deaths caused by heart disease have dropped 40% for adult women and 30% for adult men. Death from stroke has dropped 50% for both sexes.

Taxpayers finance Canada's health care system, which covers hospital and doctors' services. All Canadians, regardless of their ability to pay, have access to well-trained doctors and well-equipped hospitals; nevertheless some studies suggest lower income groups are less healthy.

Under Canada's Constitution, provinces are responsible for delivering health care, so the national system is made up of interlocking provincial health plans. Each province spends about one-third of its yearly budget on health care.

The federal government sets basic standards and pays part of the money – about 30% – needed to run each provincial health plan. It also provides health care directly to natives, members of the military and other special groups.

Health and Welfare Canada estimated that Canadians spent a total of $61.8 billion (9.2% of GDP) on health care in 1990. The United Nations' *Human Development Report 1992* showed that in 1987, the last year for which comparable figures are available for all G-7 nations, only the United States spent more of its GDP on health care.

Canadians have spent more money on health care every year since 1960, both in dollars and as a portion of the GDP.

In 1960, they paid 5.5% of the GNP for health care (GNP is very similar to GDP). In many years since, total Canadian health spending has increased more than 10%. The largest yearly increase was 20% in 1975.

Older people generally use medical services the most. As in other countries, Canada's growing elderly population may take larger amounts of doctors' and hospitals' time over the next several decades if patterns of use stay the same. In 1961, Canada's elderly population (65 and older) was 8%, and consumed 30% of all hospital days. By 1989, the elderly population was 11%, and consumed 55% of all hospital days.

Social Security   Canada's social security programs help support the elderly, the disabled, people with low incomes, and families with young children. These programs paid an estimated $69.7 billion in direct benefits in 1989-90, or about 10.6% of the GDP.

A quarter of this was aid to the elderly, including Old Age Security, Guaranteed Income Supplement and Spouses' Allowance programs. As Canada's population ages, these programs will likely consume more and more of the money the government raises through taxes.

From 1985-86 to 1989-90, spending for the Canada and the Quebec pension plans increased more than for any other program. Disability pension payments shot up 105% to $1.8 billion and retirement pension payments jumped 89% to $8.2 billion.

Federal Programs   Federal and provincial social security programs guarantee income security to Canadians.

When they were created they were universal – they paid the same benefits to everyone regardless of income – but some have been changed in recent years.

For example, universal family allowances – introduced at the end of the Second World War – were paid to all families with children under 18 years old. In 1989, the government announced it would ''claw back'' pensions and family allowance cheques of families making over $50,000. In 1992, it further announced family allowance cheques will be entirely eliminated, replaced by a child tax credit system paying benefits only to low- and middle-income families.

I remember growing up as a young lad in Victoriaville, Quebec, and playing in our back yard. I got my first pair of skates

when I was three or four years old and skated every day throughout the long winters. I remember listening to *Hockey Night*

in Canada in the 1940s, and I remember when Maurice Richard scored 50 goals in 50 games in 1945.

The next morning, we woke up and staged our own *Hockey Night in Canada*, complete with mock broadcast. But that was the

way it was in those days. We went to school, to church and we played hockey.

Jean Béliveau, born in Trois-Rivières, Quebec. Former hockey player in the National Hockey League, Member of the Hockey Hall of Fame,
Officer of the Order of Canada.

In a 1973 review of George Ryga's *The Ecstasy of Rita Joe*, a New York critic wrote: "'Canadian playwright.' The words seem a little incongruous together, like 'Panamanian hockey-player,' or 'Lebanese fur-trapper.'"

Twenty years ago, Canadian artists often found themselves treated as oddities, even at home. To both critics and audiences, "serious" art was something done in New York, Paris or London. As Robert Fulford, former editor of *Saturday Night* magazine once put it, "My generation of Canadians grew up believing that, if we were very good or very smart, or both, we would someday *graduate* from Canada."

To a generation that has grown up taking Canadian prominence in the arts for granted, such sentiments may seem incredible. But in the late 1940s, concerns about malaise in Canada's artistic community were so general that the federal government appointed the Royal Commission on National Development in the Arts, Letters and Sciences.

In its report, the commission lamented the absence of a distinguished artistic community in Canada. There were few Canadian artists and even fewer arts organizations. A deluge of artistic products were flowing into Canada from other countries, making it difficult for Canadian artists to be seen and heard.

Today, a night out in a Canadian city might mean attending a film noir set in Montreal's Vieux Port; a play set in a Cree community in Northern Ontario; or a dance collaboration involving native dancers, a Quebec City choreographer and a Hungarian-born composer. The range of Canadian cultural events has become dazzlingly wide.

This achievement has been no accident; it is rooted in the support Canada offers its artists. For more than 30 years, Canada has consciously fostered cultural development through government funding of cultural industries, through grants to individual artists and arts organizations, and through enforcing Canadian-content legislation.

In the 1980s, as Canadians spent more money on cultural activities, Canada's arts increasingly affected the economy. By 1989, almost 310,000 Canadians were directly employed in the arts sector, which contributed about $11.3 billion to the Gross Domestic Product (GDP) (2.0% of the total), compared with $5.2 billion (or 1.7%) in 1981. (GDP is a measure of the value of all goods and services produced in the economy). Related goods and services accounted for another $5.8 billion.

Remarkably, Canada's arts have matured in an era of globalization and mass communications. Foreign cultural products continue to pour into Canada, and in today's global marketplace the battle for audiences has never been so intense. Canada's arts industries – particularly film, sound recording and publishing – must compete with the rest of the world, inside and outside Canada's borders.

At Centre Stage: Canada's Performing Arts

A stage can create magic. Before the curtains rise, the air hums with creative tension. Last-minute sounds – the tuning of strings and horns, the soft shuffling of backstage performers and the low rumbling of props being pushed into place – create anticipation on both sides of the curtain. As the lights dim, and the audience settles in, the sense of expectation can be as palpable as the creative act to follow.

Every year, this moment occurs thousands of times across Canada at dance, theatre, and musical performances. Increasingly it occurs for audiences and Canadian companies beyond Canada's borders. Canadian orchestras tour Europe's musical capitals, Canadian dance companies pack halls in Japan, and Canadian theatre companies delight and amuse children throughout the United States.

Statistics Canada's annual survey of performing arts companies covers most of the country's major professional, non-profit companies. The number of performing arts organizations varies from year to year as organizations are continually being founded or folding. In 1989-90, Statistics Canada's survey included 234 theatre companies, 100 music organizations, 54 dance companies and 14 opera companies. Together, these companies staged over 40,000 performances, attracting a total audience of 13.9 million.

Theatre   In a 1979 speech on theatre in Canada, actor and playwright Mavor Moore said: "It may very well be that in time to come, the most valuable aspect of the Canadian theatre will turn out to be its difference from that of others; that it will offer the world not only an alternative North American art, but a model for greater diversity in general – because we are a pluralistic society in which no really 'national' theatre can exist nor should be expected to."

Ten years later, Moore's words ring resoundingly true. Classical theatre is kept alive in Canada by groups such as Montreal's Theatre du Nouveau Monde and Ontario's Stratford and Shaw festivals, while contemporary Canadian playwrights are increasingly recognized at home and abroad.

Many of these playwrights work in small regional and alternative theatre companies that explore Canada's cultural and social diversity. The scope for such theatre is immense. As Quebec playwright Marianne Ackerman has said, "This country has a great big frozen pack of untold stories. [If] we have difficulty as a nation [it is] because we haven't told each other [all] our stories . . . " For Ackerman, the challenge of the playwright is to "unfreeze" our rich legacy of stories. For theatre producers across the country, this process is well underway.

In the 1980s, Canadian theatre flourished with ticket sales and the number of performances rising steadily. In 1988-89, 202 non-profit companies gave over 33,000 performances for a total audience of 9.4 million. In 1989-90, as Canadians began tightening their belts in tough economic times, 234 companies

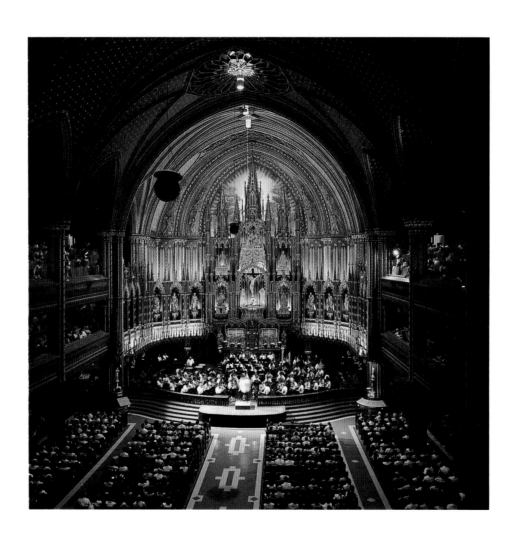

gave about the same number of performances, but attendance dropped to 8.5 million. Many theatre companies moved to fewer productions, shorter runs and higher ticket prices.

By 1990-91, economic recession and a decline in public funding increased the pressure on theatre companies. For many companies, touring is essential to developing new audiences, but the new economic climate made touring a risky business. At the same time, many small theatre groups began pooling talent and resources on collaborative productions. These collaborations help stretch scarce resources, but many directors say they suppress the creative skills of one or both of the companies involved.

In lean times, theatre directors and producers must become experts in the business of marketing theatre. Some manage to balance their creative and marketing responsibilities, but others worry about losing time needed to write and direct plays. Increasingly, new generations of writers, producers, directors and actors are challenged by the business as well as by the creativity of theatre.

Canada's pool of theatrical talent is continuously replenished by 114 universities, colleges, and private schools offering postsecondary programs in theatre arts. In 1990-91, the Canada Council – a Crown corporation that awards grants to organizations and individual artists – contributed almost $2 million in grants for professional theatre training to organizations and individuals.

Dance Dance can be delicate, subtle and discrete, or it can be athletic, flashy, thunderous. At times, it can even be disturbing. Dance in Canada ranges from the tautly disciplined performances of the Royal Winnipeg Ballet and the impassioned spirit of traditional native dance, to the leading-edge innovation of Montreal's La La La Human Steps.

Traditional repertoire is the "backbone" for many Canadian dance companies. Familiar classics such as *Swan Lake* or *Giselle* not only guarantee steady subscription revenues, they also help fund challenging and innovative modern productions.

After years of struggling to get adequate funding, training and recognition, Canada's dance community enjoyed increasing public interest and touring opportunities throughout the 1980s. Every year, new regional and national troupes have "danced" into the limelight. In 1988-89, 48 dance companies gave over 2,300 performances in Canada for audiences totalling 1.7 million.

But in 1989-90, with the beginnings of the recession, the audience for dance began to decline. Statistics Canada reports that 54 companies performed slightly more than 2,400 times for only 1.5 million people. With attendance down, many dance companies began offering smaller subscription packages coupled with more traditional repertoire.

As the number of dance companies has increased, competition for funding and audiences has become stiffer. Of all the performing arts groups, dance companies are most dependent on Canada Council funding, which has been capped since 1987.

E t adorabunt in conspectu ejus uni

versæ familiæ gentium Gloria.

GRAD

Alle lu ia ij

Jo seph fili david no li ti

mere acci pere mariam con ju

gem tuam quod e nim in e-a na

tum est de spi ritu san cto est

Al le lu ia

Sic de us dile xit mun —

dum ut filium su - um u - nige

nitum daret ut salve turmun

dus per ip sum.

PROSA

Sacræ familiæ felix spectaculum nas

centis gratiæ dulce cunabulum se nobis

referat Quis natum cogitet intactæ

virginis vitum ne territet sol puri lumi

In 1989-90, overall expenditures for small, medium and large Canadian companies were half a million dollars higher than their revenues.

In 1990-91, the Canada Council provided $2.2 million to organizations and individuals for dance training. Throughout Canada, over 30 public and private schools offered professional dance training in 1990.

Music The boundaries of musical expression have expanded relentlessly in this century. As Canadian writer Ulla Colgrass puts it, ''the combination of music, technology and nature is the auditory landscape of our age.''

In the late 1970s, Canadian composer R. Murray Schafer put this maxim into practice. In an old barn in southern Ontario, Schafer assembled a modern soundscape from a miscellany of objects old and new. A teeter-totter connects to a musical saw, a gong, and randomly arranged wires that dance across piano strings. Bells dangle from the rafters. Every object is connected to and affects the others. This musical mobile produces bangs, rustlings, hoots, and shadings of sound in between.

Schafer's point, in his compositions as well as in his soundscapes, is that any sound can be heard as music. As he explained to violinist Yehudi Menuhin in the internationally acclaimed Canadian Broadcasting Corporation (CBC) television series *The Music of Man*, ''People can be taught to listen discriminatingly, starting by making judgments about simple sounds: for instance, how many sounds you hear at a given moment.''

Canadians listen to avante-gardists like R. Murray Schafer, to rock and roll, to jazz cool and hot, to classical, to calypso, to reggae, to country, to rap – and to countless combinations of these categories.

Canadian musicians play in jazz, rock, blues and folk festivals across the country. They play classical music in theatre halls and parks. They accompany dance and theatre performances. They perform filmscores and advertising jingles. They perform in recording studios and on busy street corners. In fact, Canada has enough professional musicians to fill a small city. The Canadian chapter of the American Federation of Musicians of the United States and Canada has 24,000 Canadian members representing all genres of music.

Although many music-lovers relish the atmosphere of a live concert, a growing number opt to listen at home, often to compact discs. A generation ago, prerecorded music was a ''calling card'' for bands and orchestras hoping to lure audiences to live performances. Today, sound recording technologies may actually be competing with live performances.

For Canadian symphonies and opera companies, this is a sobering thought. In 1988-89, nearly 4,000 performances by 104 Canadian symphony and opera companies attracted almost 4 million people. The following year, 114 companies performed 4,500 times for a total audience of 3.7 million.

To encourage attendance, many companies are tending toward more conservative programming, choosing familiar foreign classics over innovative works by Canadian composers. Of all the performing arts groups, large-sized opera companies showed the greatest surplus over expenditures in 1989-90.

At the time *Canada: A Portrait* went to press, the long-term effects of the 1990-91 recession on music and opera companies were unclear. But, faced with increased costs and declining attendance, many companies have been forced to shorten their seasons or cut musicians' salaries – or both.

Contemporary Visual Art   Contemporary visual art in Canada is both experimental and innovative. It often challenges traditional values, ideals and even the nature of art itself. From the fringe to the mainstream, Canadian artists explore everything from intensely personal thoughts to social and political issues. And in this exploration, they use an incredible array of materials and media.

For years, contemporary artists in Canada had few choices: they either worked in isolation, far from the hub of artistic activity, or they moved to major cities where they could become part of an artistic community. Many contemporary artists worked in seclusion, with few opportunities to interact with their counterparts in other regions of the country. As some contemporary artists moved toward more experimental and interdisciplinary techniques, they could not rely on existing galleries and institutions to support their efforts.

By the early 1970s, contemporary and alternative artists began organizing a ''living network'' of artists' centres across the country to provide opportunities for artistic events, exchanges and debates. In 1976, 15 artist-run centres – then known as ''parallel'' galleries – met for the first time with the Canada Council to discuss funding.

Today there are about 100 artist-run centres in Canada, comprising a strong sector in the arts community. For many independent artists, these centres provide a fertile training ground, a place to meet with colleagues and the public, and a forum for presenting works in progress and completed works. Indeed, many artists and curators now in major institutions received their ''field experience'' at artist-run centres. Many centres run exchange programs with artists from other countries. Some offer resource centres, libraries or video-editing facilities; others deal with specific art media, such as print or performance art.

In 1990-91, 72 artist-run centres shared $3 million in funding from the Canada Council. Artist-run centres are also supported in part through provincial or municipal grants. Even with government grants, many centres depend on dedicated volunteers and fundraising events to support themselves. For example, many centres in Ontario have taken advantage of charity bingos, raising close to one-fifth of their total funding.

Preserving the Past: Canada's Heritage

At the Royal Tyrrell Museum of Palaeontology in Drumheller, Alberta, you can stare into the jaws of a Tyrannosaurus rex,

Art is not interested in art, art is interested in life.
— STEPHEN VIZINCZEY, 1986

King of the Dinosaurs. In downtown Ottawa's Canadian War Museum, you can step into a World War One trench. In Quebec's Place Royale, you can sip café au lait where Jean Talon, the first intendant of New France, once strolled the narrow 17th century cobblestone pathways.

Canadians are fiercely proud of their roots. From coast to coast, almost 2,300 public and private heritage organizations chronicle Canada's social, economic, and political legacies. In 1989-90, almost 114 million visits were made to Canada's museums, archives, galleries, planetariums, observatories, aquariums, zoos, botanical gardens and nature parks. That year federal, provincial and municipal governments spent $1.1 billion on heritage activities.

Once commonly perceived as monolithic buildings filled with dusty glass showcases, museums have become bustling cultural centres. Canada's national museums have worldwide reputations for innovation and accessibility: visitors can stroll through exhibit halls, attend film screenings, lectures and other cultural events — they can even rent museum halls for weddings and other special events.

Some Canadian museums have actually dispensed with walls. ''Ecomuseums,'' or living museums, bring entire communities together to preserve their heritage. An ecomuseum can be a region, a village, a street, or a building. The ecomuseum for the Cowichan and Chemainus valleys in British Columbia preserves the spirit of an entire region: visitors can hike along old logging trails, stroll along the docks at the Tall Ship Museum at Ladysmith, visit the native arts centre at Duncan or explore the archaeological digs at Cowichan Bay's abandoned logging camps.

Dozens of Canadian communities have created their own ecomuseums with help from Heritage Canada's *Main Street Canada* program, which encourages revitalization projects in traditional downtown areas. By sprucing up older downtown buildings, the Main Street program has given a face-lift to urban businesses and provided new homes for local cultural and performing arts groups. Besides increasing community pride and heritage awareness, ecomuseum projects boost economies by helping to create local tourism industries.

A Native Renaissance   In the words of writer Heather Robertson, ''If survival is the dominant theme of Canadian life, the native people are already mainstream. They have survived against all odds and expectations, and their will to live has given them a new and enormous creative momentum.''

Native communities across Canada are reclaiming their birthright. This has meant reviving native languages and spiritual practices, preserving the knowledge held by elders, and re-interpreting traditional art forms from basket-decorating to story-telling. Native Canadians are also creating new art forms by blending their native traditions with arts disciplines that have traditionally been part of western culture. Architect Douglas Cardinal designed the widely acclaimed Museum of Civilization, in Hull, Quebec.

Cultural Ambassador or Cult Phenomenon?
American author Mark Twain called her ''the sweetest creation of child life yet.'' The Japanese call her ''Akage no An'' (Anne of the Red Hair). Whatever she is called, the fictional character out of Lucy Maud Montgomery's 1908 novel *Anne of Green Gables*, is the basis for an entire cultural industry. Montgomery published several more Anne novels, a TV film and series has been produced, and sales of Anne collectibles such as cookbooks, toiletries and perfume are estimated at $5 million. Montgomery's books have been translated into more than 20 languages, and read by more people than any other Canadian story. Montgomery's childhood home in Prince Edward Island, the setting for the Anne stories, draws almost 300,000 visitors annually, of which 8,500 come from Japan alone.

Playwright Tomson Highway's works *The Rez Sisters* and *Dry Lips Oughta Move to Kapuskasing* have met with rave reviews across the country, and have won major awards. And composer and conductor John Kim Bell has built a solid reputation for his innovative and impassioned productions combining native music and rhythms with classical choreography.

Literature and Publishing

Margaret Atwood has written, ''Literature is not only a mirror; it is also a map, a geography of the mind.''
Canadian writing can take you from a fishing village on the rugged Newfoundland coast to a cafe in Vancouver's bustling Chinatown; from an Inuit community on the ice-locked shores of Baffin Island to a small-town church in rural Saskatchewan. And many first- and second-generation immigrant Canadian writers reach beyond Canada's borders to Africa, Asia, Latin America, and the Caribbean.
In the 1990s, Canada's literature is as diverse and multicultural as Canadian society. English-Canadian, French-Canadian, aboriginal, and other Canadian writers are all expressing distinctive visions of Canada, and are sharing these visions with a growing readership.
Books   The 1980s were boom years for Canadian literature and publishing. New writing talent emerged from every corner of Canada's ethnic mosaic and the publishing sector became

a highly creative, regionally diverse, risk-driven industry – an impressive achievement in a market increasingly dominated by multinational companies.

Over the past 20 years, Canadian-owned publishing houses have diligently nurtured Canadian authors – these houses now produce 80% of Canadian-authored books. In 1989-90, over 90% of the 302 publishing companies with revenues over $50,000 were Canadian-owned. That year, over 6,000 new Canadian titles were released, and sales of Canadian books had increased from the previous year at double the rate for other books. Of $1.4 billion in domestic and international book sales, Canadian titles represented slightly over one-third.

Yet foreign books continue to dominate Canada's market, creating fierce competition for Canadian publishers. A handful of foreign companies control over 50% of the English-language market, dominating the most lucrative areas in the industry: educational publishing and commercial import distribution. Through vigorous marketing, these companies have set standards in consumer taste, retail pricing and consignment selling. Some Canadian firms act as agents for imported titles, using the revenue to subsidize Canadian titles, but an increasing number of U.S., British and French publishers have set up branches to sell directly to Canadian buyers, depriving Canadian publisher agents of vast quantities of business.

Reading Canadian

- **Canadian writers are regularly nominated for the Booker McConnell Prize, one of the world's most prestigious literary awards.**
- **Canadians have won both the Prix Goncourt and Prix Medici in recent years.**
- **Farley Mowat's *Never Cry Wolf* has sold over 1 million copies in the former Soviet Union alone.**
- ***Anne of Green Gables* is read by virtually every high school student in Japan.**
- **In Spring 1991, the *New York Times* reviewed an Alice Munro collection of short stories, adding, ''Thank God for Canadian writers.'' The *Times* went on to say that without them, the American spring fiction season would have been dull and lifeless.**

The French-language sector of Canadian publishing is slightly more secure. In 1989-90, Canadian-owned French-language firms held 83% of the market, accounting for total domestic sales of $161 million, compared with $34 million for foreign-controlled firms. Language barriers protect the French market against a profusion of U.S. products; and the cost of shipping books from France, combined with stringent policy measures taken by the Quebec government, work in favour of Quebec publishers.

Globalization and mass-market publishing threaten to undermine what the Canadian industry has built over the past 20 years — a market for books written by Canadians, for Canadians. Four Canadian-owned publishers went out of business in 1991, and one of the larger companies cut its previously impressive fiction list to a mere handful of titles. Many companies laid off staff.

What's Ahead   The 1990s may be tough for many Canadian publishers. In the face of a recession and the new Goods and Services Tax, many are calling upon the federal government to re-examine legislation covering foreign ownership and exports. They are also calling for industry and government to work together to help Canadian companies compete more effectively in a global environment.

In January 1992, the federal government announced plans to spend $140 million over five years to help strengthen the Canadian book publishing and distribution industry.

Periodicals   Canadian periodicals cover everything from sports to survey methodology; indeed, lined up side-by-side, these titles would fill a magazine shelf almost half a kilometre long. Canadian publishers produce magazines for almost every economic, professional, artistic, scholarly, religious and recreational community in the country.

In 1989-90, a reported 1,494 Canadian periodical titles were in circulation, compared with 1,100 in 1984. Sixty percent of these were published in English, 22% in French, and almost 15% were bilingual. The remaining 3% were in languages other than English and French. Canadian periodical publishing accounts for about 4,500 full-time jobs and almost 1,800 part-time jobs, and $170 million in wages.

Unlike book publishers, Canada's periodical publishers are mainly Canadian-controlled. Of 1,091 periodical publishers in 1989-90, less than 1% were foreign-based. And of $903 million in revenues reported that year, just 5% went to foreign firms.

In 1989-90, the combined annual circulation of Canadian periodicals dropped to 522 million copies, down 6% from the previous year. Yet despite decreased circulation, periodical revenues rose 5% from the previous year to $891 million, mainly because of increased advertising revenues. Total expenses also increased by 5%, leaving profit before taxes at 4% – the same as in 1988-89.

Canada has a major trade deficit in periodicals, and this imbalance has widened over the years. In 1980-81, imports totalled $277 million in current dollars, while exports totalled $53 million. By 1988-89, imports had almost doubled to $510 million, while

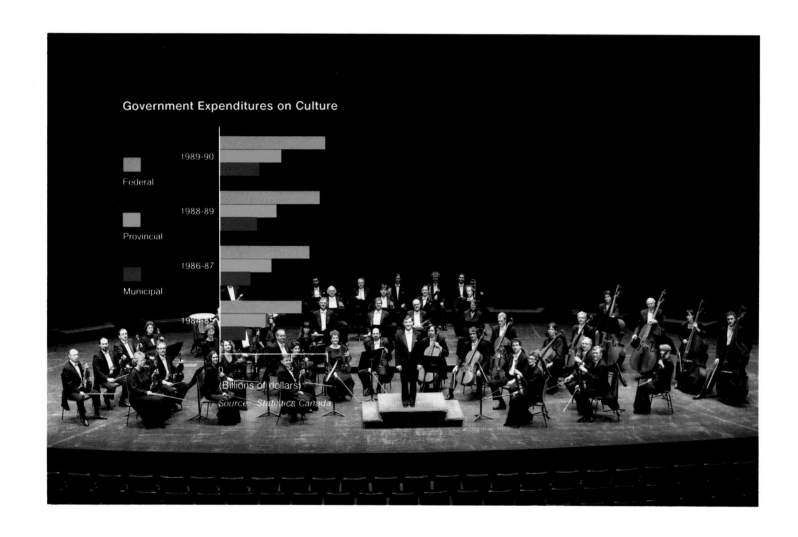

exports increased by only 9% to $58 million, leaving a deficit of $452 million in current dollars.

U.S. companies have a great deal of influence in the English Canadian market. Newsstand space is reserved for vigorously marketed best-selling magazines, which are usually American. Hence Canadian publishers generally distribute their products by mail, which is more costly and takes longer. Furthermore, U.S. magazines have become the price-setters, setting a ceiling on what Canadian companies can charge for similar English-language magazines that are more costly to produce.

Although English-language periodicals account for almost two-thirds of all Canadian periodicals, the number of French-language and bilingual (French and English) magazines has increased rapidly in the past few years. Between 1985-86 and 1988-89, the number of French-language periodicals climbed 26% to 339, and bilingual publications rose 87% to 247, compared with English-language periodicals, which increased a modest 3% to 901.

Increasingly, publishers, especially in Quebec, are entering into partnerships with foreign companies to produce new magazines. These arrangements reduce the risks and costs inherent in launching new consumer periodicals.

Advertising sales are the main source of revenue for the industry. To help Canadian periodicals compete, the Income Tax Act forbids Canadian companies from claiming ads placed in U.S. magazines as business expenses.

In late 1989, the federal government began phasing out Canada Post's periodical subsidy program. In 1991, postal rates for most Canadian publishers jumped by 50%. The new 7% Goods and Services Tax and an economic recession put further stress on Canadian book and periodical sales.

Going to the Movies

Canadians love movies! In 1989-90, feature film attendance at theatres and drive-ins was 82.1 million, and home video rentals generated an estimated $1.2 billion. Yet because Canada is the largest export market for U.S. films, audiences rarely see Canadian productions. Canadian feature-length films account for less than 5% of the theatrical market and 10% of the home entertainment market.

Distribution is critical to the film and video industry. As the "gatekeepers" between producers and their audiences, distributors wholesale to exhibitors, videocassette retailers, television broadcasters, cineclubs and libraries.

Years ago, the major Hollywood studios established their own distribution branches to control the release of their films in Canada. Yet these U.S. film giants rarely invested their Canadian profits in Canadian productions. Admissions paid by Canadian filmgoers have helped to finance decades of U.S. film production, but have contributed almost nothing toward creating an authentically Canadian industry. In 1990, out of a total of 144 distributors

that responded to Statistics Canada's annual survey, 23 were foreign-controlled and accounted for 62% of Canadian distribution revenues.

In 1989-90, Telefilm Canada – a Crown corporation with a mandate to strengthen the competitiveness of Canadian films – devoted $12.8 million to the Feature Film Distribution Fund, which enables distributors to help finance Canadian feature film production.

Canadian distributors handle 95% of Canadian theatrical films, of which there were less than 50 in 1991, but cannot survive on these revenues alone – they depend on additional revenues from independently produced foreign films. Only 19% of films distributed by Canadian-owned companies in 1989 were Canadian.

Because of its French-language market, Quebec has not been as thoroughly integrated into the Hollywood marketing system. With less competition from the south, the Quebec film industry started earlier and has progressed further than that of English Canada. In the early 1980s, U.S. firms began distributing non-American, French-language films in Quebec, taking a vital supply source away from Quebec distributors. In 1983, the Quebec Cinema Act was passed to license and regulate film and videocassette distributors in the province. Regulations set out by this Act led to an agreement with U.S. distributors whereby Quebec-based distributors would control distribution rights to non-English language films, allowing the U.S. companies to distribute the same English films they distribute in English Canada.

Cameras Rolling! In 1989-90, 48 theatrical feature films were produced in Canada, compared with only 16 in 1984-85. This rapid growth was largely due to private investment incentives such as the Capital Cost Allowance (CCA) program, offering a 100% tax deduction for investment in Canadian productions. In 1988, when the tax credit was reduced to 30%, private investment came to a virtual halt.

The major market for Canadian films and television programs is domestic television, particularly the publicly owned CBC. Many productions sold to TV thus depend on public funding and on government policies. Telefilm Canada provided funding for 40% of English and 20% of French prime-time drama in 1988-89. And from 1984-85 to 1988-89, changes in Canadian-content regulations helped increase viewing of prime-time Canadian programming by 30% on English-language stations, and by 28% on French stations. Many Canadian television series have reached international audiences through sales to the United States and to European countries.

Canadian producers are reaching wider audiences through production partnerships with other countries. So far, Canada has signed co-production agreements for film or television programs with 19 countries. Managed by Telefilm Canada, these agreements allow co-productions to be certified as domestic productions for both partner nations. In 1989-90, Telefilm invested $9.2 million in eight official co-productions with France

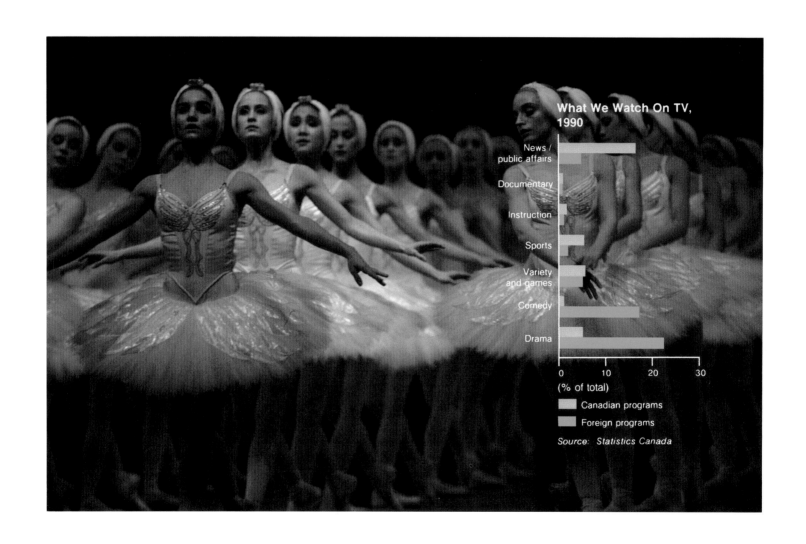

What We Watch On TV, 1990

News / public affairs
Documentary
Instruction
Sports
Variety and games
Comedy
Drama

0   10   20   30
(% of total)

Canadian programs
Foreign programs

Source: Statistics Canada

(5), Yugoslavia (1), Great Britain (1), and the Soviet Union (1). Not all components of the Canadian film industry depend upon public funding or legislation. One of the most lucrative areas for the industry is television commercials. In 1989-90, almost 5,000 commercials were produced by Canadians, an increase of 8% over the previous year. Yet revenues in the same period dropped from $143 to $134 million, possibly because market fragmentation has made television a less efficient advertising medium.

Coming Soon... International co-productions are likely to be increasingly common. The critically acclaimed 1991 film *Black Robe* – a co-production between Canada and Australia – offered compelling incentive for future feature-length collaborations for Canada's independent filmmakers.

International collaborations on television series have proven to be a stable and profitable production market. Broadcasters worldwide are linking up with foreign partners to ease the burden of rising production costs. This broader television market means opportunities for Canadian producers, but possibly at the expense of Canadian content.

B r o a d c a s t i n g

Tuning in... If there is one thing Canadians have in common, it's television – over 98% of the country's nine million households have at least one TV set.

But in the 40-odd years since the CBC transmitted its first television signal, TV has undergone a drastic transformation. Cablevision and converters, pay TV, specialty channels and VCRs together mean a startling range of viewing choices – yet Canadians are actually watching less than they were a decade ago.

In 1990, Canadians spent an average of 23.3 hours each week watching TV – the latest in a series of declines from a high of 24.3 hours six years earlier. Children and teenagers in particular are watching less. When Canadians *are* tuned in, 40% of their time is spent watching foreign-produced drama or comedy. Canadian-produced news and public affairs are also popular, accounting for more than 16% of viewing. Altogether, just over two-thirds of viewing time is spent on foreign (mainly U.S.) shows, over half of which come through Canadian stations.

For many years, private television broadcasters in Canada carried mostly imported U.S. programming. When cable companies began importing entire U.S. networks into the country, the federal government introduced Canadian-content legislation to strengthen Canada's production industry.

To be considered Canadian, a television program must score a minimum of six out of 10 points. Two points are given each for a Canadian director or writer. Single points are assigned for cast and production positions. Yet Canadian-content legislation and public financing may soon lose their effectiveness. In 1992, four pay TV and 13 specialty channels were operating in Canada – in 1982, when the Canadian Radio-television and

Telecommunications Commission (CRTC) began licensing these channels, only two pay TV channels existed. Specialty channels did not arrive until 1984. As domestic television services expand, the result is smaller audiences and increased competition and production costs.

The CBC – Canada's largest public network – is by far the most important source of Canadian programming for both French and English audiences. The CBC accounts for just over one-quarter of all production in Canada and is the major buyer of independently produced Canadian programs. Parliamentary funding for the CBC has decreased considerably in the past few years, causing it to depend more and more on advertising revenues.

Conventional broadcasters are seeing their profits shrink as increased viewing choices have fragmented both audiences and advertising dollars. Broadcasters can no longer depend on programs that appeal to a wide range of tastes, because advertisers prefer reaching smaller, targetted audiences.

Canadian broadcasters and cablevision companies are also concerned about direct broadcast satellites, poised to leave the launch pad some time in 1993. Known as "deathstars", these high-powered satellites may soon beam over 100 foreign channels into receiving dishes no larger than the lid of a garbage can, potentially thwarting 40 years of regulation aimed at nurturing Canada's domestic industry.

The good news for Canadian broadcasters is . . . the news. A 1991 Environics survey showed that 70% of Canadians say television is their primary news source – a 20% increase since 1969. In 1988, the CBC launched Newsworld, Canada's first 24-hour all-news channel. By the mid-1990s, CTV – Canada's largest private broadcaster – also expects to have its own round-the-clock news service.

Because news is far cheaper to produce than original drama or comedy, and because it is 100% Canadian, networks will likely expand news programming well into the 1990s.

The Art of Radio For many people, Canadian culture *is* CBC Radio, the national public network. The CBC's AM and FM networks feed fast-breaking news, public affairs, cultural events, sports and entertainment to listeners from coast to coast, from the far North to the U.S. border and beyond. Broadcasting in English, French and several aboriginal languages, the CBC is available to 99% of Canadians.

The CBC first broadcast in 1936 and radio drama quickly became the country's national theatre, and as public interest in drama grew, scores of Canadian theatres – including Ontario's Stratford Theatre – were established. In the same way, generations of Canadian writers were nourished by commissions from the CBC. And as a major vehicle for Canadian music, the CBC has introduced hundreds of Canadian performing and recording artists to the public.

Canadians also listen to more than 500 private radio stations offering a mix of music, news, weather and sports. A highly competitive business, private radio relies mostly on advertising for revenues. In 1989-90, private stations reported revenues of $770.4 million.

Private AM and FM radio stations are licensed by the CRTC. The formats of these stations include adult contemporary, middle-of-the-road, country, album-oriented rock, and so on. Most stations must have at least 30% Canadian content in their broadcasting.

For a song to qualify as Canadian content, it must meet two of four criteria: (a) the principal performer is Canadian; (b) the lyric writer is Canadian; (c) the music composer is Canadian; (d) the song was recorded in Canada. Many well-known foreign artists meet the requirement by recording songs with lyrics and music by Canadians.

AM radio in Canada has been hit particularly hard by audience fragmentation. More and more AM listeners are tuning into FM stations for better sound quality, and advertisers are following the audiences. FM stations are not allowed to sell as much advertising time as AM stations, yet they bring in roughly equal advertising revenues. Many small AM stations have either applied for FM licenses or have stopped broadcasting altogether.

Sound Recording   The music industry is a tough business. A young musician who dreams of accepting a Juno Award on national television needs a rare combination of creativity, ambition and good luck. A music career can be as short as a hit song, or as long as the reigns of perennial favourites such as Bruce Cockburn, Stompin' Tom Connors, Rita MacNeil, Joni Mitchell, Anne Murray and Ginette Reno.

The success of these latter artists, both in Canada and internationally, may be encouraging to aspiring pop stars. Every year, more Canadian performers hit the top of the pop charts in Canada, and go on to enjoy wide recognition in the United States and overseas.

One of the biggest Canadian names in pop music in 1991 was Bryan Adams, who was nominated for seven Juno Awards in Canada, six Grammy Awards in the United States and who played for wildly enthusiastic crowds across North America and Great Britain. Singer Roch Voisine has been similarly embraced by young audiences across Canada and in France. Quebeckers were proud when Celine Dion was cited as Female Vocalist of the Year at the 1991 Juno Awards, and they were elated when she sang live for audiences around the world at the 1991 Academy Awards.

Canadians are among the world's greatest consumers of pre-recorded music. But the old adage ''music is a universal language'' rings particularly true in Canada: of 4,289 albums released in 1989-90, only 615 had certified Canadian content. Despite the abundance of Canadian talent, Canadian record labels must struggle against high unit costs and a market crowded with imported products. Of 186 record producers in 1989-90, less than 8% were foreign-controlled, yet these firms garnered slightly over 86% of total revenues of $635.6 million.

Government financial assistance to the sound recording industry is modest in comparison with other cultural industries. Some provinces, notably Quebec, support special promotional projects, chiefly through subsidies to companies and to trade associations for marketing, promotion and production. The federal government supports the industry and helps establish Canadian musicians by maintaining Canadian-content quotas for broadcasters.

The Canadian Radio-television and Telecommunications Commission requires that Canadian music occupy at least 30% of broadcast time on all AM and FM stations. The one exception is FM classical music stations, which are required to broadcast 10% Canadian content. In 1986, Communications Canada introduced programs worth $5 million annually to help fund Canadian-content sound recording masters and music videos, to improve the professional skills of industry employees, and to expand marketing in Canada and abroad.

The private sector also promotes Canada's sound recording industry. The Foundation to Assist Canadian Talent on Record (FACTOR) gives grants or forgivable non-interest loans covering up to 50% of production costs for English-language artists whose work has commercial potential. To qualify under the program, the artist, producer, and record label must all be Canadian; at least 50% of the lyrics must be written by a Canadian; and the master must be wholly produced in a Canadian studio. Projects are assessed by representatives from radio stations across Canada. Musicaction, a similar organization for French-language artists, was established in Quebec in 1985. Both organizations receive funding from Communications Canada.

Using Our Leisure Time

When Canadians aren't using their leisure time to attend movies or the theatre, watch television or listen to music, they're probably out exercising.

Throughout the 1980s, Canadians became increasingly aware of the benefits of exercise. Average household expenditures on sporting and athletic equipment increased 6% between 1982 and 1990. And in 1991, 32% of Canadians said they were "physically very active," compared with 27% five years earlier. In 1988, the Campbell's Survey on Well-Being in Canada found that 79% of Canadians over the age of 15 spent at least three hours a week on some form of physical activity, up from 57% in 1981. More Canadians were scheduling weekly physical activities ranging from aerobic workouts to team sports. In fact, participation in all of the most popular activities had increased – with the exception of jogging.

Favourite Activities   Walking was the most popular exercise in 1988, attracting 63% of Canadians aged 10 or over. Gardening was next (50%), followed by swimming (42%), bicycling (41%), social dancing (33%) and home exercise (31%). About 20% of Canadians went skating, jogging or running, downhill skiing or golfing. More men than women participated in gardening, skating, downhill skiing and jogging, while women led the way

in walking, swimming, dancing and home exercise. Canadians usually exercise outdoors (32%), at home (28%), at a fitness club or community centre (26%), or at school or work (10%). For many people, exercise is social – 37% of Canadians exercise with friends, and 23% with family members, classmates or co-workers. Another 35% exercise alone.

Amateur Sport – Competing at Home and Abroad   For generations, amateur sport has been an integral part of Canadian life. Thousands of Canadians play team sports such as soccer, baseball, softball or lacrosse, while others compete against their own personal best by running marathons or taking aerobics classes. Countless Canadians volunteer their time and expertise as coaches and organizers for amateur fitness and sports groups.

The natural extension of this passion for sport is Canada's national training program for gifted athletes. Co-ordinated by Sport Canada, a federal government agency, this ''core support'' program helps pay for professional, technical and coaching staff, and defrays the costs of meetings, coaching clinics and seminars, and national and international competitions.

This kind of backing has helped Canada place strong teams at major international sporting competitions such as the Olympic, Pan-American, Commonwealth, and World University games. Since 1980, Canadians have been world champions or world record-holders in alpine skiing, speed skating, figure skating, yachting, track and field, equestrian events, swimming, trap shooting, boxing, wrestling and the pentathlon.

The 1992 Winter Olympics   For many Canadians, hockey is *the* test of national grit. And even though the Canadian team lost to the Russian team in the battle for gold at the 16th Olympic Winter Games in Albertville, France, the silver medal they brought home signified the most successful Winter Olympics ever for Canadian athletes.

Canada took seven medals – two gold, three silver and two bronze – matching the country's previous best performance at the 1932 Winter Olympics in Lake Placid, New York.

Gold medalists in 1992 included Calgary's Kerrin Lee-Gartner for women's downhill skiing, and Quebec's Sylvie Daigle, Angela Cutrone, Nathalie Lambert and Annie Perreault for women's short-track speed skating in the 3000-metre relay. Silver medals went to Team Canada for hockey; to Montreal's Frederick Blackburn for men's 1000-metre short-track speed skating; and to Frederick Blackburn, Michel Daignault, Sylvain Gagnon and Mark Lackie for men's short-track speed skating in the 5000-metre relay. Bronze medals went to Isabelle Brasseur and Lloyd Eisler for pairs' figure skating, and to Myriam Bédard for the women's 15-kilometre biathlon.

Of the 117 Canadian athletes participating in the Games, 60% finished 16th or better in their events, up from 50% at the Calgary Winter Games in 1988.

Canada also performed well in demonstration sports – events that may eventually become full Olympic competitions. Canadians won a demonstration gold and a silver for men's aerial freestyle skiing and a bronze for women's curling.

ℐisions of ℰanada

In this 54th edition of *Canada: A Portrait*, we are pleased to introduce a new feature: a gallery of selected Canadian contemporary art, as a companion piece to our expanded chapter on the arts and leisure in Canada.

Contemporary art in Canada is as varied and diverse as the people who live here. The 10 visual artists' work presented here constitutes a brief survey of visual art, chosen to include a wide representation of artists, men and women, from different parts of Canada. The glimpse of contemporary art this survey provides reminds us that Canadian artists are deeply attached to the landscape and the history of our regions.

This art gallery includes the works of both well-established and new Canadian artists who investigate identity and convey a sense of social vision. In one way or another, these images speak of both a personal and a national vision. For example, in Dennis Tourbin's visual poem, we are presented with a witty ramble of ways to look at Canada. In Gathie Falk's painting, there is a veneration of the ordinary that celebrates aspects of daily life. Carl Beam shares a vision of memory and identity from his own personal history. In Eleanor Bond's work, viewers are invited to imagine the look of an economic future that is different from the present. The photographs of Claude-Philippe Benoit darkly contrast scenes of human organization and images of a natural order. The personal and poetic visions of artists such as Marlene Creates, Betty Goodwin, and Serge Tousignant could also be said to describe a social imagination.

To insist on seeing works of art as the expression of a social vision is not to demand too much. Cultural activity is always engaged in social structures and even a highly personal exploration of vision becomes social when shared with an audience. The best art of our time will examine, challenge and question our preconceptions. The subject of art is properly the human condition in all its aspects of beauty, doubt, pain and pleasure.

One of the important roles of artists is to create a sense of personal and national identity for the community of people where they live. It is through our culture and our cultural diversity that we *imagine* ourselves. The greatest gauge of societies in history has been their cultural achievements. Even as our artists help bring to Canada a rich cultural diversity from around the world, contemporary artists of our time will be part of the measure of how Canada is seen in the future.

A vision of Canada is a unity of many views. Each person's view is coloured by the filters of experience and perspective. Exploring these views through a selection of images of contemporary Canadian art provides a collection of perspectives.

Certainly as the question of our identity has been of consuming importance to us as Canadians, these artistic images form an interesting and challenging contribution to an overall portrait of Canada.

Betty Goodwin Born: Montreal, Quebec, 1923. Lives in Montreal. *Swimmer Series: Untitled*. 1982. Oil, oil pastel, pencil on paper, 46 x 71 cm. Collection of the Department of External Affairs, Ottawa.

This drawing is from a compelling series of heroic works by Montreal artist Betty Goodwin in which a swimmer is depicted struggling in water. Viewed from below, head unseen above the water's surface, the swimmer flails arms and legs, awkwardly thrashing, almost drowning. In spite of the lush and beautiful drawing, an atmosphere of peril surrounds the struggling figure. The artist has drawn veils of colour in mysterious depths, creating an enclosing and enveloping space for the isolated swimmer.

Eleanor Bond Born: Winnipeg, Manitoba, 1948. Lives in Winnipeg. *IV. Converting the Powell River Mill to a Recreation and Retirement Centre*. From the *Work Stations Series*. 1985. Oil on canvas, 248 x 360 cm. Collection of the Canada Council Art Bank, Ottawa. (Photograph courtesy of the artist).

Eleanor Bond states that she makes paintings that are ''fictional and somewhat narrative, in the future sense.'' Her recent paintings are about the nature of community in urban centres, and about issues of leisure, parks and recreation.

The *Work Stations Series* are visionary landscape paintings of a future where urban space and ''country'' collide. Among the subjects of these works are unemployment, displacement and dislocation as the symptoms of widespread socio-economic upheaval. Surprisingly, these imaginary scenes are not without a wry humour.

Serge Tousignant Born: Montreal, Quebec, 1942. Lives in Montreal. *L'identité*. 1986. Colour photograph, 127 x 01.6 cm. (Photograph courtesy of the artist).

In his studio the artist has drawn geometric figures directly on the wall, arranged suitcases, boxes, packing crates and other elements, then carefully lit the scene to compose and take the photograph. Beside the reference to personal identity, which is the sense one has of oneself and where one belongs, the title also refers to the concept of geometric identity: where one figure is identical to another if, after transformation in space, the two can be traced upon each other. The persuasively real space of the photograph is a fictional diagram to find one's way home. The crates and boxes, the props in this photographic ''set'', evoke the idea of a move, *déménager*, and a voyage.

Claude-Phillipe Benoit Born: 1953. Lives in Montreal, Quebec. *Untitled diptych #3.* 1989. From the series *Intérieur,*

jour. Silver prints, 79 x 215 cm. (Photographs courtesy of the artist).

In this series of paired photographs, Claude-Philippe Benoit is using a strategy of direct comparison to point at similarities between

the realm of the 'natural world' and the order of the human workplace. The diptych compares a scene of lush dark rainforest

from the West Coast of Canada, with the interior of an old manufacturing business in Central Canada. It is a study in notions

of vitality and decay, order and chaos, prevailing darkness and remote light. The forest represents the natural order; and the

factory is an example of a certain manner of civilization and of how humans organize their world. In each picture of the pair

there is an impression of chaos and tangle, yet each scene also resonates in different ways with an underlying sense of purpose

and order.

Lorène Bourgeois Born: Boulogne Billancourt, France, 1956. Canadian landed immigrant, 1989. Lives in Toronto,

Ontario. *La Bête*.1987. Monoprint, etching inks on BFK paper, 228 x 183 cm. (Photograph courtesy of the artist).

Lorène Bourgeois creates her art with a unique technique involving the assembly of monoprinted sheets to make a large composition.

The sources for some of her images are old photographic archives. While working in Banff, Bourgeois found old photographs

of the standing bear and the bathing woman. The comparison and contrast of these two figures invites speculation about the

differences between the two subjects, and a consideration of what may be their similarities. It is the artist's delight to cause the

viewer to wonder what is going on in the picture, what menace, what dialogue.

Carl Beam Born: Manitoulin Island, Ontario, 1943. Lives in Peterborough, Ontario. *Neo-Glyph-2*. 1984. Watercolour and coloured pencil on paper, 101 x 105 cm. Collection of the Canada Council Art Bank, Ottawa.

The sequence of images of a black flying bird shows an event in time, shows how time changes. This bird is a powerful symbol.

Neo-Glyph-2 is an artwork about identity and time. The reproduction of a photograph of a white missionary, native people, and settlers, freezes a moment of a previous time. It is a memory, a still souvenir of a past existence. The animal skull is a sign of previous life, and another image of power. The imprint of a hand is like a signature, a living presence, here repeated twice to mark a sequence, to write again of change and identity.

Marlene Creates Born: Montreal, Quebec, 1952. Lives in St. John's, Newfoundland. *Seven Stones Set Adrift*. 1985.

Photograph/landwork. (Photograph courtesy of the artist).

In this series of artworks, Marlene Creates performs personal and poetic gestures in the landscape, and photographs the results.

Though the photograph is exhibited in art galleries, it is the creative action performed alone in the landscape that is the essential

artwork. The photograph records a transitory and temporary sculpture. The title of *Seven Stones Set Adrift* describes the gesture

the artist has performed, selecting seven stones from the shore of an inlet in Baffin Island and setting them on a piece of ice to

drift away to where the current will take them.

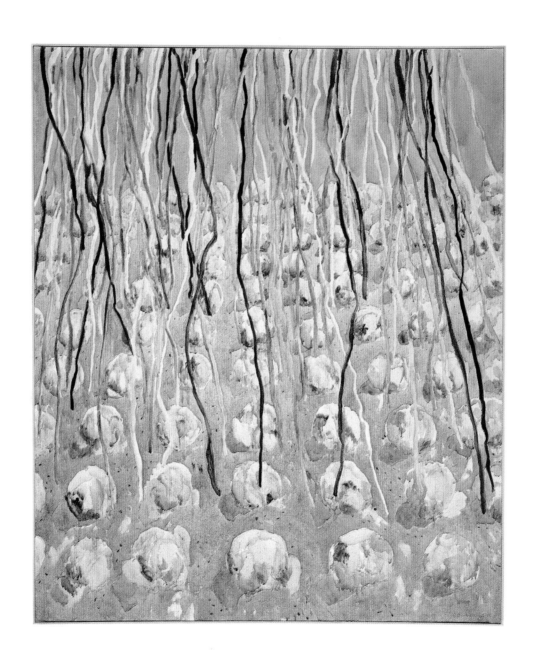

Gathie Falk Born: Alexander, Manitoba, 1928. Lives in Vancouver, British Columbia. *Theatre in b/w and Colour: Yellow Cabbages with Ribbons*. 1983. Oil on canvas, 198.1 x 167.6 cm. (Photograph by Trevor Mills, courtesy of the Art Gallery of Greater Victoria).

One of the themes of Gathie Falk's art is the ''veneration of the ordinary'': the presentation of normally unheroic aspects of everyday life as significant events. In this painting the artist presents a simple garden of ordered rows of cabbages decorated with coloured ribbons. She gives it an important status as an oil painting, as 'theatre' for the celebration of the domestic garden and for the beauty of colour and light. While there is often a sense of absurdity in Falk's work, she also combines an affectionate humour with a celebration of the values of ordinary life. It is in this valourization of domestic virtues that Gathie Falk's art can be understood to express a social vision.

Wanda Koop Born: Vancouver, British Columbia, 1951. Lives in Winnipeg, Manitoba. *Untitled*. 1990. Acrylic on plywood, 244 x 244 cm.

While this painting by Wanda Koop appears to be a sketch of a scene, it is also a gesture of an urban mood. Culture and nature are conflated in a direct and free manner in the medium of acrylic paint on two sheets of primed plywood. A skyline of buildings is integrated with its water reflection. A fluid blue, representing and describing states of nature, is spread dripping and blurring across the surface of the painting. Vivid flashes of hot colour break through the blue. Koop's paintings integrate images of the structures of human organization, in this example city buildings and decorative patterns, with signs of vigour, life and essential forces of nature.

Dennis Tourbin Born: St. Catharines, Ontario, 1946. Lives in Ottawa, Ontario. *Canada Is.* 1991-92. An ongoing visual/literary artwork.

This visual/literary artwork by Dennis Tourbin is a *visual poem*, especially produced for inclusion in this edition of *Canada: A Portrait.* Beyond simply being an illustrated text, Tourbin's piece is an imaginary, charged poetic field of communication cross-fire on the subject of Canadian identity. *Canada Is* is a synthesis of colour, words and literary images concerning issues of contemporary cultural identity, social style, and history. Through the poetic device of metaphor, Tourbin is sharing with us what Canada means to him.

CANADA IS A TOOTHPICK ON THE DASHBOARD OF A PICKUP TRUCK. CANADA IS THE LONELINESS OF A LONG DISTANCE FOLK SINGER. CANADA IS A BROWN TROUT IN A FIELD OF MINT. CANADA IS A COLORFUL TREE. CANADA IS AUTUMN. CANADA IS AN AMERICAN DREAM. CANADA IS A FLOOR FILLED WITH PEANUT SHELLS IN A HOCKEY ARENA. CANADA IS A TABLE FILLED WITH BEER. CANADA IS A DEER STANDING IN A FIELD. CANADA IS A LAST CIGARETTE. CANADA IS SCRAP METAL. CANADA IS A PINE TREE — BURNING. CANADA IS A MINNOW IN A METAL BUCKET. CANADA IS A FOREIGN FILM. CANADA IS A FOREIGN FILM WITH SUBTITLES. CANADA IS A NEXT DOOR NEIGHBOR. CANADA IS A CROW ON A HIGHWAY

*V*iewing Canada from space on the voyage of Discovery provided a perspective from which all Canadians can learn more about each other, our land and our relationships with the rest of this world. It is so beautiful – the crisp white mountains, the freedom of the prairies, snow-filled valleys, dark blue lakes, and coastlines that surround us from one side to the other – a continuum of strong geological features that unify our land. I am proud to be a Canadian, proud to have represented our country on an international mission to space. We are a very special people.

Roberta Bondar, born in Sault Ste. Marie, Ontario. Neurologist, educator, Canadian astronaut, second Canadian in space and first Canadian woman in space.

*T*HE *E*CONOMY

On the rocky, barren north shore of Great Slave Lake in the Northwest Territories, a team of miners rides a kilometre deep shaft into a gold mine. At the same moment, in a towering office building on Toronto's Bay Street, a broker accepts a client's order for stock in the company employing the miners. Thousands of kilometres away, a receptionist in Halifax, Nova Scotia, sends a call forward on a Canadian-made telephone switching device containing circuits printed with gold from the Great Slave Lake mine.

Canada's economic life is built on countless interactions like these, shaping every aspect of our lives. Indeed, with one of the most diverse and productive economies in the world, we have an impressive range of economic choices, both as workers and as consumers. The strength of our economy has allowed us to develop social programs and services – our medical and unemployment insurance programs, for example – that rank among the best in the world.

Moreover, Canada has had one of the fastest growing economies of the major industrialized nations since the end of World War Two. Canadians are among the wealthiest people on earth, with one of the highest levels of per capita Gross Domestic Product (GDP is a measure of the value of all goods and services produced in the economy). In the 1990s, Canada has been recognized by both the Organization for Economic Co-operation and Development (OECD) and the World Bank as one of the strongest contenders in the global marketplace.

Yet like other industrialized nations, Canada has not been immune to economic problems. Individual and regional income disparities persist; government debt has reached high levels; and growth in productivity for a number of Canadian industries slowed in the 1980s. These long-term problems were compounded in 1990-91 by a recession that brought high unemployment, record personal and business bankruptcies, and large-scale restructuring in business at a time of high government deficits.

Despite the strain of this recession, Canada's long-term economic future seems very promising. Canada has a highly skilled and educated workforce, an enviable record of creating jobs, a thriving export sector, and strength in high-growth sectors such as telecommunications, aerospace and high-tech manufacturing.

This chapter presents an overview of Canada's economic life in the 1990s – what we produce, where we work, what we earn, and how we spend and save. It also surveys the economic diversity among Canada's regions, and concludes with a look at trends in Canada's economic life.

Canada's Key Economic Players

In a newspaper cartoon by Alan King of the *Ottawa Citizen*, a man is standing in an amusement park in front of a huge rollercoaster ride called ''THE ECONOMY''. The operator, explaining how the ride got its name, points out: ''Well, we tried to come up with a name that would really *scare* people.''

As King's cartoon suggests, the state of the economy is central to our lives. It can affect our jobs, where we choose to live, our standard of living – and yet many people find it complex, even mysterious.

How does the economy work? Economic life involves thousands of decisions, regulations and financial transactions, but its day-to-day workings are largely shaped by four major players: government, business, consumers and our major trade partners.

Government   Canada's federal government is a key player in managing the national economy. It influences Canada's interest and exchange rates (through the Bank of Canada), regulates industry and trade, sets tax rates, and with the provinces helps fund the basic services – such as education and health care – that support Canadian society. Federal and provincial governments also build roads, bridges, airports and other infrastructure underpinning Canada's economic development.

Besides influencing Canada's overall economic environment, governments have an immense direct effect on spending and employment. In 1991, Canada's municipal, provincial and federal governments spent about $357 billion – more than one-half of total GDP. In the same year, government employed some 1.5 million Canadians – more than 10% of the total work force.

Federal government departments fund research in the national interest. For example, data collected by Statistics Canada are used to calculate the national unemployment rate, GDP and the inflation rate – essential economic indicators. Many government departments and agencies – notably the National Research Council and Industry, Science and Technology Canada – conduct and fund research and development that helps Canadian industry become more competitive. Other departments – such as Consumer and Corporate Affairs Canada and Employment and Immigration Canada – regulate and monitor business and the labour market.

On occasion, governments enter the market economy directly by setting up a Crown corporation. These corporations – Canada Post and Via Rail are federal examples – operate by the rules of the market economy, but are ultimately responsible to Parliament. In 1991, there were 35 federal and 131 provincial Crown corporations, employing about 300,000 Canadians.

Canada's governments supply a wide range of services – but at a price. In 1991, total government taxation revenue amounted to almost $247 billion – about $9,000 for every Canadian.

More than half of Canada's tax revenue goes to individual Canadians through programs such as veterans' benefits, unemployment insurance payments and family allowances. Governments at all levels use tax revenues to support the disabled, the chronically ill, the unemployed, the elderly, and others in need. Many Canadians feel that this comprehensive social "safety net" is the embodiment of our national ethic.

The federal government also redistributes resources among the provinces and territories. Federal taxation revenues collected in the more prosperous provinces – such as Ontario, British Columbia and Alberta – are transferred to less prosperous

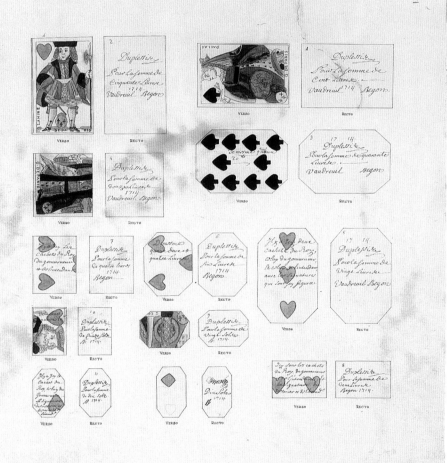

provinces: for example, Quebec and the Maritime Provinces. These transfers ensure that all Canadians, regardless of their income or where they live, have access to comparable health care, education and other government services.

Business Like other major industrialized countries, Canada has a market economy in which most decisions about production, incomes, consumption, capital formation and prices are made by individuals and individual businesses.

A major engine of Canada's economy is its businesses, of which there are more than a million. From family farms and corner convenience stores to multinational corporations, these businesses organize production and take the risks that go with producing goods and services. They also employ the majority of Canada's workforce.

Business investment – in construction, machinery and equipment and other capital expenses – plays an important role in creating jobs and fuelling economic growth. However, this investment is highly volatile, influenced by consumer demand, interest rates and both short- and long-term economic prospects. For example, business investment dropped from 21.5% of GDP in 1981 to 16.5% in 1984 – a difference of several billion dollars – in the wake of a major recession.

Many Canadian businesses are owned or controlled by foreigners, although foreign ownership has declined considerably in recent decades. In 1968, for example, foreign control accounted for 57% of Canadian manufacturing and more than 80% of the petroleum and gas industry. By 1984, a decade after the federal government introduced stricter foreign investment regulations, foreign control had dropped to 48% of Canadian manufacturing and 36% of petroleum and gas. Although investment regulations were relaxed considerably in 1985 and withdrawn altogether under the Canada-United States Free Trade Agreement in 1988, foreign control has remained relatively stable.

Canada's businesses compete to get consumers to buy their goods and services. To do this, they increase efficiency, introduce new products, find ways to make existing products more appealing, and market and advertise.

This competitive environment means that Canada's economic landscape is always changing. During boom times, for example, businesses often expand rapidly – but in a downturn, they may be quickly whittled down.

Competition also shapes the labour market. As certain industries decline and others emerge, so do different types of jobs. For example, the increase in computers and telephone answering machines has decreased the demand for traditional office support staff, while creating demand for computer technicians, programmers and sales people.

At the heart of Canada's economic life is its financial sector. Canada's 10 chartered banks are among the country's largest financial institutions, financing business start-ups and expansions and helping consumers buy goods.

In 1991, Canada's banking system consisted of 10 Canadian-owned banks and 56 foreign-owned banks. At that time, their total assets were valued at $612.0 billion – $426.1 billion in Canadian dollars and $185.9 billion in foreign currency.

Other financial institutions include trust and mortgage companies, credit unions and caisses populaires as well as consumer loan, life insurance, and investment companies.

As well as borrowing from banks, Canada's businesses and governments raise capital in Canada's stock and bond markets. In 1990, the value of shares traded on the Toronto and Montreal stock exchanges – far and away the largest of Canada's five stock exchanges – was about $80 billion. This was a drop of more than $20 billion from 1989 – an example of the volatility of stock markets. The provinces and the federal government issued close to $50 billion in bonds in 1990, while corporations issued about $15 billion.

Consumers Consumers are the common denominator of economic life – their changing tastes and priorities determine what businesses produce, where they locate, and how they develop over time. In 1990, Canadian consumers spent about $400 billion – nearly two-thirds of GDP, and almost $15,000 per capita.

Consumer spending is highly sensitive to changes in the economy. Rising unemployment or interest rates, new or increased taxes – all of these can dampen spending on all but essential goods and services.

In tough economic times, such as the 1990-91 recession, governments may try to tempt consumers to spend by offering tax breaks and other incentives. In 1992, for example, the federal government lowered the minimum required down payment for homes financed by the Canada Mortgage and Housing Corporation from 10% of the purchase price to 5%. At the same time, the rules governing Registered Retirement Savings Plans (RRSPs) were changed, allowing consumers to borrow from their RRSPs to finance home down payments for first-time buyers.

Canada's Trade Partners Canadians don't even have to leave home to recognize the importance of trade to our lives. On a typical working day, we may awake to an alarm clock made in Taiwan, get out of a bed made in Burlington, Ontario, and for breakfast perk coffee grown in Brazil.

We sell more than a quarter of our goods and services abroad, and we import commodities and manufactured goods from around the world.

Trade connects us to an international marketplace, allowing us to specialize at what we do best. For most of our history, this has meant exporting natural resource products such as lumber, minerals and wheat. Natural resources are still important to Canada's trade – accounting for about 40% of total exports in 1991 – but Canada's image as a "hewer of wood and drawer of water" is becoming outdated. Canada has a diverse non-resource manufacturing sector, responsible in 1990 for 17.9% of GDP and 37% of exports. And Canada is a world leader

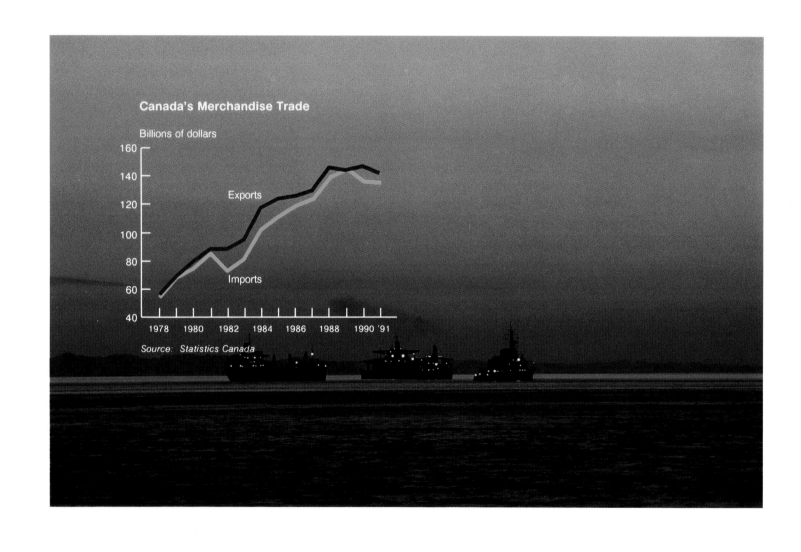

Canada's Merchandise Trade

Billions of dollars

Exports

Imports

Source: Statistics Canada

in such high-tech, high-growth areas as telecommunications, space sciences and technology, nuclear power technology, remote sensing, bioengineering and geophysical exploration. At the heart of Canada's trade is our special relationship with the United States. As United States President John F. Kennedy said in an address to Canada's Parliament in 1961: "Geography has made us neighbours. History has made us friends. Economics has made us partners."

Canada and the U.S. share the largest two-way trade in the world. Three-quarters of Canada's exports go to the U.S., and the U.S. in turn supplies three-quarters of Canada's imports. Canada-U.S. trade amounted to CDN$189 billion in 1991, well ahead of U.S.-Japan trade of about CDN$150 billion. And the share of Canada's exports sold to the U.S. increased from 66% in 1970 to 76% in 1991. After the United States, Canada's largest trading partners in 1991 were Japan ($17.36 billion), the United Kingdom ($7.10 billion), Germany ($5.85 billion), France ($4.02 billion) and South Korea ($3.97 billion).

In the past decade, Canada has experienced an export boom. Our exports increased 10% annually from 1980 to 1990 – faster than every other major industrialized nation except Japan. Despite this growth, Canada's share of world exports dipped from 5.3% in 1970 to about 4% in 1989, largely because of rapid economic development in other parts of the world, such as the Pacific Rim.

Canada's largest export is automotive products, accounting for about one-quarter ($32.1 billion) of all exports in 1991. The other major exports are all natural resource products, which together account for more than 40% of Canada's exports – one of the highest rates of any industrialized nation. Canada's most important natural resource exports are wheat, crude oil, lumber, pulp and paper, and metals.

Although natural resources still dominate Canada's exports, manufactured goods are catching up. Manufactured end products accounted for 47% of total merchandise exports in 1990, up from 32% in 1980. The most important contributor to this steep climb, after automotive products, has been exports of telecommunications and related equipment, worth $4.7 billion in 1991. Canada has also retained its status as a leading exporter of aircraft and railway equipment.

Canada imports mostly manufactured end products – machinery and equipment, electronic goods, computers, consumer items. In 1990, Canada ran a trade deficit in end products of $24 billion.

Canada generally runs an annual surplus on merchandise trade, but in recent years, our overall trade position has been eroded by persistent deficits in non-merchandise trade – particularly interest payments required to service our growing international debt. In 1991, Canada's exports exceeded imports by more than $7 billion, but the current account balance was –$26.7 billion.

A basic factor influencing Canada's trade in natural resources is the classic law of supply and demand: when demand for a commodity exceeds supply, the price rises; when supply exceeds demand, the price drops.

For Canadian natural resource exporters, this translates into often volatile markets. During economic slowdowns, numerous suppliers vying for shares in a shrinking market leads to over-supply, and hence declining prices. Indeed, low commodity prices in 1990-91 were an important factor in Canada's recession – especially in their negative impact on corporate profits.

Demand for Canadian manufactured exports is influenced by factors such as foreign exchange rates and Canada's labour costs relative to other countries.

To maintain their traditional export markets, many Canadian firms must compete with producers in emerging nations – many of which have considerably lower labour costs. Canada must also compete with other highly industrialized countries, all striving to become more productive and efficient.

The value of the Canadian dollar relative to other currencies can affect trade in manufactured goods. When the dollar becomes more expensive in terms of other currencies, Canadian exports become more expensive in world markets (or the profits from exports decline), and imports into Canada become cheaper; when the dollar declines, the opposite occurs.

Trade policies are another crucial factor. Since the 1950s, the world trend has been toward gradual elimination of tariffs and other trade barriers. Examples are the establishment of the inter-national GATT (General Agreement on Tariffs and Trade) and the 1992 economic integration of the countries of the European Economic Community (EEC). Closer to home, the 1988 Canada-United States Free Trade Agreement called for virtually complete elimination of tariffs between the two countries by 1998. And in 1992 discussions were underway between the United States, Mexico and Canada for a comprehensive North American Free Trade Agreement (NAFTA).

An Economic Overview

Economic Growth and the 1990-91 Recession Canada's economic growth since the 1950s has been remarkable, averaging over 4% in the 1950s and 1960s, and over 3% in the 1970s. Despite slower growth in the 1980s, Canada's GDP climbed steadily from $19.1 billion in 1950 to $649 billion in 1989, with real growth every year except 1982.

This impressive performance has given Canada the seventh-largest economy of the western industrialized nations after the United States, Japan, Germany, France, the United Kingdom and Italy. Yet in 1990, after eight years of economic growth, Canada slid into its second recession within 10 years.

Generally, recessions are marked by sluggish demand for goods and services and increased unemployment. Although they bring hardship, some economists argue that recessions can have the positive economic effect of relieving inflationary pressures by reducing demand and spending. Such reductions can put the economy in a position to grow and produce more in the future.

Recessions occur periodically as part of the ''business cycle,'' the ups and downs in economic activity over time. The 1990-91 recession was Canada's ninth since the end of World War Two. Previous recessions have lasted an average of 10 months.

Most OECD countries were also in recession by 1991, although Canada's downturn was one of the most severe. Ontario was hit particularly hard, suffering a greater decline in economic activity and employment than in the 1981-82 recession.

The recent slump was quickly reflected in the labour market – employment dropped nearly as fast as output, and Canada's unemployment rose well above the OECD average. By the end of 1991, GDP was 1.5% lower than in 1990.

One unusual feature of the 1990-91 recession was that household savings remained stable; they increased in most of Canada's earlier recessions. Another feature was the unusual rise in productivity in manufacturing.

By early 1992, a number of positive developments were at work in the economy. Exports climbed by over 10% in the first three months of the year, interest rates were at their lowest level in almost two decades, and inflation remained at historically low levels. However, the unemployment rate remained at about 11%, with firms continuing to be cautious about hiring. As a result, incomes remained weak, as did consumer confidence in the short-term economic future. Because consumers account for about 60% of GDP, compared to 30% of GDP for exports, it was still unclear whether the economy had begun to emerge from the recession.

Employment and Unemployment   Canada's economy produces many things, one of the most important of which is jobs. From 1960 to 1990, jobs in Canada more than doubled – the best showing of any OECD country. Canada achieved this thanks to strong economic growth and a dynamic and flexible labour market. The next highest increases were 79% for the United States and 41% for Japan. European OECD countries trailed with an average increase of 15%, with Germany, France, Italy and the U.K. all falling below this average.

In Europe, slower growth in jobs meant a larger increase in unemployment than in Canada and the U.S. From nearly full employment in the early 1970s, average OECD unemployment rose by some three percentage points by the end of the 1980s. Canada's increase was less than two points, while Europe's was between five and six points.

The reasons for the Europe/North America employment divergence have been much discussed by economists. The OECD Secretariat has cited rigid European labour laws that discourage hiring and firing. Partly as a result of these laws, layoffs are more common in Canada and the U.S. during economic slumps. However, job growth in North America accelerates faster when the economic cycle turns up.

Even at the best of times, Canada has high rates of job turnover. In 1988, near the peak of the most recent economic expansion,

almost 1.2 million Canadian workers were permanently laid off, and another 600,000 were laid off temporarily – yet overall employment posted a gain that year.

And Canada's high rate of layoffs in the 1980s did not lead to high unemployment. The United Kingdom and France had fewer layoffs, but their unemployment was higher because spells of unemployment lasted longer. Less than 10% of the unemployed found a job each month in France and the U.K., compared to almost one-half in the U.S., and one-third in Canada. Consequently, long-term unemployment (12 months or longer) accounted for over 50% of unemployment in Europe, compared to less than 10% in Canada and the U.S.

Because Canada's labour force has grown even faster than the number of jobs, the unemployment rate has tended gradually upwards since the 1960s. (The unemployment rate is an estimate of the percentage of the labour force unemployed and seeking work. The measure doesn't account for the so-called "hidden unemployed" – those who would like to work but have stopped searching for work because they believe none is available. In 1992, this group comprised about 550,000 Canadians.) In 1969, Canada's unemployment rate was 4.4%. Ten years later, it had climbed to 7.4%. During the 1981-82 recession, it peaked at 11.8%, dropping to 7.5% in 1988. In late 1990, unemployment once again began to climb, reaching a high of 11.1% in March 1992.

Inflation, Interest Rates and the Bank of Canada   The Bank of Canada – the government's central bank – isn't a bank in the usual sense: the average Canadian can't open an account there. As an agent of government, the Bank of Canada controls the supply of money and credit in Canada, and thus affects levels of spending and economic activity.

The bank implements monetary policy through its control of the money supply – the cash and liquid deposits held by Canadian households. The bank exercises its control primarily through the chartered banks.

The source of this control is the Bank Act's requirement for the chartered banks to keep a percentage of their deposit liabilities as cash reserves to cover potential demands for withdrawals. The reserves may be held as deposits at the Bank of Canada or as holdings of currency. Chartered banks use their cash reserves in excess of the minimum requirements to make loans and expand their assets and liabilities – in other words, to "create" money. However, this ability is limited by the total amount of cash reserves available.

Every week, the bank administers the "bank rate" (the rate at which it is willing to lend money to the commercial banks), which in turn affects the interest rates that Canada's commercial banks charge businesses and individuals.

Of course, the bank's policies are not the only influences on Canada's interest rates. To attract investment, Canada's rates must compare favourably with those of the United States and other industrialized countries. The value of Canada's dollar

relative to other currencies also affects our interest rates. Canada's interest rates have fluctuated considerably in recent decades. A quick survey of five-year intervals makes this plain: On November 12, 1970, the rate was 6.00%; on September 3, 1975, it was 9.00%; by December 31, 1980, it had climbed to a near-record 17.26%, but by December 25, 1985 it had dropped to 9.49%. Recently, the rate has been at its lowest level in 20 years, dropping to 6.50% in May of 1992.

The Bank of Canada's policies on interest rates can have a major impact on inflation, which occurs when prices rise, causing the relative value of money to fall. Inflation can slow economic growth because the unpredictability of future prices may cause businesses to shy away from long-term investments.

Controlling inflation is a major aim of Canada's federal government, although inflation's causes and cures are the subject of debate among economists, politicians and academics.

The rate of inflation – as measured by the Consumer Price Index – has varied considerably over the past 30 years. The lowest increase was 0.8% in 1961; the highest was 12.4% during the 1981-82 recession. When the 7% Goods and Services Tax was introduced in January 1991, inflation briefly jumped from 5.6% to 7.0%, but the recession brought a dramatic decline – by March of 1992, the rate was at 1.6%. This was the second lowest inflation rate in the OECD, after New Zealand at 0.8%.

Investment   Foreign direct investment has always played a major role in Canada, especially that of U.S.-based multinational companies. From 1960 to 1988, however, Canadian investment abroad began to catch up, jumping from about 20% of foreign investment in Canada to over 50%. Because this investment shift is part of the worldwide move to a more globally-integrated economy, it may be accelerated by the signing of the Canada-U.S. Free Trade Agreement.

As Canadian direct investment abroad has risen, our reliance on foreign direct investment has dropped from 51% of all investment in Canada in 1970 to only about 25% in 1990. The difference has been made up by purchases of bonds, up from 29% of total investment in 1970 to about 50% in 1990. This is noteworthy for at least two reasons. First, bondholders do not take an active role in managing a company, unlike direct investors. Second, a steady stream of interest payments to bondholders leaves the country every year.

In 1990, foreign investors held 38% of all Government of Canada bonds. Total interest payments abroad amounted to $17 billion, at an average interest rate of 9.3%.

Canada's Diverse Economic Landscape

Canada's economy features striking regional diversity. Manufacturing is heavily concentrated in Central Canada, while the eastern and western regions depend on primary industries such as forestry and agriculture. Services are more evenly distributed across the country.

Regional Employment by Sector, 1991

% of total employment

80

60

40

20

0

| Atlantic Provinces | Quebec | Ontario | Prairies | British Columbia |

Primary/construction   Manufacturing   Services

Source: Statistics Canada

Three-quarters of Canada's manufacturing jobs and almost 70% of its financial industry are located in Central Canada (Ontario and Quebec), but less than 50% of Canada's primary industry is in this region.

Ontario has by far the largest and most diversified economic base of all of Canada's provinces. In 1989, it accounted for 41.5% of Canada's GDP, or $270 billion. It is the largest producer and employer in all major industries, even in resource-based industries such as mining and agriculture.

Because of this diversification, no one industry dominates the province's economy, as agriculture does on the Prairies. Auto production is the largest manufacturing industry – more than 90% of Canadian auto production is located here. In addition, much of Canada's production of machinery and capital goods comes from Ontario. Most of Ontario's exports – especially automobiles – are shipped to the United States. In 1989, passenger auto exports alone accounted for close to $14 billion, or 21% of the province's total exports.

Quebec's economic structure is similar to Ontario's, but the nature of Quebec's manufacturing base is different. Food processing dominates, and Quebec makes most of Canada's textiles and clothing. Pulp and paper, smelting and refining also play a large role. In 1989, newsprint was Quebec's top export, accounting for $2.8 billion, or 11.8% of the province's total exports. A larger proportion of Quebec's exports go to Europe than do Ontario's exports.

The economies of the western provinces – British Columbia, Alberta, Saskatchewan and Manitoba – rely mainly on primary industries. Agriculture alone – particularly Saskatchewan's grain industry – accounts for one in 10 jobs on the Prairies. Wheat was Saskatchewan and Manitoba's largest export in 1989, accounting for 32.7% of Saskatchewan's total exports, or $1.5 billion, and 11.2% of Manitoba's total exports, or $324 million.

Alberta accounts for the bulk of Canada's crude petroleum and natural gas production. In 1989, these commodities accounted for close to half of the province's total exports, or $6.3 billion.

British Columbia's resource base is forestry and metal mining. In 1989, forest products such as lumber, softwood and wood pulp accounted for more than 43% of the province's total exports, or $7.7 billion. British Columbia's role as a port of trade for goods travelling to and from Pacific Rim countries and the west coast of the United States is reflected in the size of its transportation industry, the largest in Canada.

As does British Columbia, the Atlantic Provinces of Nova Scotia, Prince Edward Island, New Brunswick and Newfoundland rely largely on mining, fishing and forestry. The Atlantic Provinces' large transportation industry is based on their access to the Atlantic Ocean. The Atlantic Provinces have the largest public sector relative to population of any region in Canada, partly because of persistently high rates of unemployment. The commercial services sector is proportionally the smallest of any region. In 1989, transportation equipment accounted for 16.9% of Nova

Scotia's total exports, or $356 million. In the same year, Prince Edward Island's top export was potatoes and other vegetables, accounting for 50% of the province's total exports, or $80 million. New Brunswick's leading export was wood pulp, accounting for 23.6% of the province's total exports, or $715 million. Newfoundland's largest export was petroleum and coal products, accounting for 28.2% of its total exports, or $516 million.

In Canada's North, resource extraction is the major industry. In the Northwest Territories, the single largest contributor to the GDP is mining (42.2%), while in the Yukon it is the second largest (20.2%) after public administration (29.4%). The top export from both territories is the same: zinc in ores, concentrates and scrap. In the Northwest Territories, it accounts for 77.6% of total exports, or $64 million. In the Yukon, it accounts for 72.6% of exports, or $168 million.

Our Economic Life

Where We Work   For decades, Canada has been gradually shifting toward a "white collar" or service economy. In the early 1970s, 37% of Canada's employment was in the goods-producing industries (which include manufacturing, construction and natural resource commodities). By 1991, the goods-producing share of employment had dropped to less than 27%.

As goods-producing employment (which tends to be dominated by "blue collar" occupations) has declined, service sector employment has soared. Nearly three-quarters of working Canadians were employed in the services sector in 1990 – almost nine million people. Almost half worked in community, business and personal services (an important sector that includes health and education). Another 2.1 million (18% of all Canadian workers) were employed in trade.

Not surprisingly, most new jobs in Canada come from the service sector. From 1970 to 1979, services accounted for 79% of employment growth, climbing to 94% from 1980 to 1989. Growth in the community, business and personal service sector has been particularly strong.

As the 1990-91 recession demonstrated dramatically, higher education is key to finding work in the service economy. Overall employment in Canada fell by about 1% in 1991, but the number of jobs for people with university degrees rose by 4.1%. Jobs for people with only a high school diploma fell by 0.8%, while jobs for people with only some high school education dropped by 5.5%.

Canada's employers are demanding high levels of education and training because these are key to increasing efficiency and innovation – crucial factors in an increasingly competitive environment.

Who works in Canada has changed as much as the jobs we do. From 1966 to 1991, Canada's participation rate – the percentage of people either working or seeking work – climbed

from 57% to 66.3%, largely because of an unprecedented influx of women into the labour market. Indeed, participation for men actually dropped slightly, from 80% to 76%. For women, the rate jumped from 35.4% to 58.2%.

Growth in the number of Canadian workers has outpaced job creation since the 1960s. As a result, Canada's unemployment rates have been higher than those of other industrialized countries. Even in the boom years of the late 1980s, unemployment was several percentage points higher in Canada than in the U.S., Japan and many European Economic Community countries. Hence reducing unemployment, particularly in regions with chronically higher-than-average rates, has been one of the perennial challenges for Canada's governments.

What We Earn Canadians are among the highest-paid workers in the world. However, in the 1980s average after-tax family income in Canada stayed at essentially the same level – just over $40,000 – for the first time in decades.

From 1971 to 1979, this average climbed 22%. After-tax data for earlier decades are not available, but average pre-tax family income jumped 27% in the 1950s and 34% in the 1960s.

It's not possible to point to a single cause for the "hold-steady" pattern of the 1980s, but the 1981-82 recession and tax increases both played a part.

In Canada, taxes on higher-income earners and government transfers to low-income Canadians help cut income disparity. For example, the poorest 10% of Canadian families accounted for only 0.4% of incomes in 1989 before taxes and transfers, but after taxes and transfers this jumped to 2.9%. Similarly, taxes and transfers reduced the share of income going to the richest 10% from 26.0% to 22.0%.

In Ontario and Quebec, which account for about two-thirds of Canada's GDP, per capita disposable incomes have grown at about the Canada average since 1961. Western Canada, producing about 30% of Canada's GDP, recorded a slightly slower increase than the national average, largely because of weakness in its natural resource industries in the 1980s. Atlantic Canada was the only region to post above-average income growth, despite producing only 6% of Canada's GDP.

What We Buy Mortgage and car payments, clothes and school supplies for the kids, heating and water bills, appliances, long-distance telephone calls – for most Canadians, the necessities of life have become much more than just food, clothing and shelter.

Over the short term, how much Canadian consumers spend on specific items varies according to the state of the economy, to changes in supply and demand (and hence to prices), and to unpredictable factors like weather – a very cold winter, for example, means higher home-heating costs.

Over the longer term, Canadian families are spending a decreasing proportion of their incomes on food, clothing and health care, and a larger portion on housing, transportation and recreation.

Canada on the Move

If the world's most varied terrain did not make the challenge of transportation pivotal to Canada, the country's sheer size would. Moving people and goods between regions is costly but vital to the nation's social and economic life.

In 1988, Canadians owned more than 12 million passenger cars. Annual spending to build and maintain roads was close to $6 billion.

In addition, intercity buses earned total operating revenues of $333 million in 1988, and the Canadian urban transport industry earned total operating revenues of $2.6 billion.

Behind the Wheel

Cars and mobility go hand-in-hand in Canada, the world's third-largest exporter of automobiles after Japan and Germany. Canadians make about 90% of their domestic passenger trips by car. Only two OECD countries (the United States and Japan) have more kilometres of road than Canada does.

In 1990, almost half of the almost $400 billion Canadian consumers spent went to Canadian retail stores. Most of the rest went for services such as plumbing, car repairs and haircuts. Housing costs – including rents – accounted for the single-largest share of consumer spending, at about 19% ($75.3 billion). Food for home consumption was next at 11% ($43.4 billion), followed by spending on restaurants and hotels at 6% ($25.3 billion). Auto sales ($19.5 billion in 1990) are not the largest component of consumer spending, but they account for much of the year-to-year fluctuation: consumers can postpone spending money on vehicles, but not on housing and food.

Other major consumer expenditures included financial, legal and other services ($22 billion); clothing ($18.3 billion); recreational and camping equipment ($15.4 billion); and gasoline and motor oil ($12.4 billion).

Government Expenditures and the ''Tax Bite''

Former prime minister John Turner once remarked, ''running a country is not like running a business. The business of business is money and profits, return, productivity. The business of politics is people.''

That governments are in the ''people business'' is borne out by the fact that more than 50 cents of every federal dollar spent on programs goes to individuals, whether in veterans' benefits, unemployment insurance payments or family allowances.

The government funds these programs through our taxes, which also support defence, education, health care, law courts and

judges, fire departments, and transportation and communication networks – things that might not be provided adequately in a strictly free market economy.

Federal government spending in 1991-92 is projected at $159 billion, compared to revenues of $128.5 billion. The government will thus run a deficit of $30.5 billion.

Since the mid-1970s, Canada's federal government has consistently run annual deficits. By 1990, the accumulated federal debt had climbed to about $400 billion. The size of this debt – more than 50% of GDP – and its continuing growth concern many Canadians.

But for governments, the debt trend is difficult to reverse. In 1991-92, for example, the federal government would have run a budget surplus – if it weren't for interest payments on the debt, accounting for 27 cents of every federal dollar.

The rest of the government's 1991-92 budget, or $115.8 billion, went to programs and operations, including $40.5 billion for old age security, unemployment insurance, family allowances, and veterans' benefits; and $37 billion in cash transfers to provincial, territorial and municipal governments. Other projected spending included $13.5 billion in industrial and regional development, science and technology, energy and transportation, and other

major transfers; and $4.8 billion for major Crown corporations. Defence cost $12.7 billion, and official development assistance $2.8 billion. The costs of running the day-to-day operations of the federal government were $18.4 billion – just under one-sixth of all program spending.

The largest single source of government revenue projected for 1991-92 is personal income taxes ($61.5 billion), followed by the Goods and Services Tax ($16.4 billion), unemployment insurance contributions ($16 billion), other revenues ($11.3 billion), sales and excise taxes and duties ($10.5 billion), and corporate income tax ($8.4 billion). Corporate tax revenue was unusually low in 1991-92 because of record low levels of profit.

Where federal taxes come from has shifted since the 1970s. In 1991-92, personal income tax generated a projected 48% of federal revenue, up from 39% in 1974-75. Unemployment insurance contributions climbed from 6% of revenues in 1974-75 to 12.5% in 1991-92, while the share of corporate income taxes dropped substantially – from 17% to 6.5%.

Canada's provincial governments in 1991 raised more than $138 billion and spent about $148 billion. Local governments raised about $56 billion and spent about $51 billion.

*M*y vision of Canada is inextricably linked with the land where I grew up, more than 1 000 kilometres north of Winnipeg. Its vastness, its immense skies, its many lakes, sandy beaches, pristine forests have all informed my plays, my writing . . . the way I see Canada and the world.

We are an enormously privileged people to live here in this beautiful country. We must treat this land of ours with respect and with deference. To me, the land is as animate and as living, as complex as any human being. Our future lies as much in partnership with this land as it does in our partnerships with each other.

Tomson Highway, born in Brochet, Manitoba. Aboriginal playwright, director and actor, nominee for the Governor General's Literary Award, recipient of two Dora Mavor Moore awards.

CANADA IN THE WORLD

The people of Brazil have a slang expression for electrical lighting: "Turn on the Canada." The Polish have a phrase for financial success: "To have Canada." And people in Yemen bake their bread with "Canada" – their name for wheat.

These expressions say a lot about Canada, and even more about how the world views the second-largest country on earth. And for good reason: Canada's reach is global. A Canadian firm built the municipal electrical utilities in São Paulo, Brazil, in 1899; Canadians opened the first McDonald's Restaurant in Moscow in 1989; Canada has the world's largest pulp and paper manufacturer, baker, shoe maker and distiller.

Canada has a reputation as a land where dreams come true. Canadian inventors – many of them immigrants – gave the world insulin, the electron microscope, the snowmobile, even the zipper. Every year, thousands of immigrants put Canada at the top of their priority list.

But Canada is perhaps best known as a peacekeeper and generous donor of food and aid. Canadian troops have served on United Nations (UN) peacekeeping missions for the past 40 years, and Canada grants refugee status to a greater proportion of its applicants than other countries do with theirs.

Canada also has its share of concerns and challenges. Canadians worry about their economy and the country's ability to compete in a globalized market. We worry about public finances, and whether Canada's many levels of government can continue to provide the social services for which Canada is renowned. And we are concerned about the environment, and the possibility that our children will inherit an ecologically damaged planet as a result of the excesses of contemporary society.

This chapter introduces a wide-angle-lens view of Canada in the world of the 1990s, in terms of our economy, our trade patterns, international investment, our use of energy, our cultural and leisure habits – even our use of drugs. It also shows Canada's role in the world community including our economic co-operation with other nations and our role in international development assistance and peacekeeping.

Canada's Economic Impact

Canada grows, mines, processes, designs and manufactures everything from wheat that resists disease to communications satellites. Canada's economy is a western industrialized economy – of such economies, it has the seventh-largest in the world after those of the United States, Japan, Germany, France, Italy and the United Kingdom.

Canada is also one of the 24 industrialized countries of the Organization for Economic Co-operation and Development (OECD). The OECD countries share several economic and demographic characteristics, but developing countries – such as India, China and Brazil – have different economic and demographic profiles.

The World Bank estimates that three-quarters of total world

output originates in the OECD countries. Of these countries, the seven with the largest economies (the United States, Japan, Germany, France, Italy, the United Kingdom and Canada) are known as the Group of Seven (G-7). They account for over 60% of total world output, and 80% of OECD output. Although Canada is the smallest of the G-7 nations in population (27.3 million), its level of per capita Gross Domestic Product (GDP) was $24,881 in 1990; this was the second-highest level in the G-7 after the United States. (GDP is a measure of the value of all goods and services produced in the economy).

The OECD notes that Canada has traditionally had one of the most prosperous and fastest-growing economies in the industrialized world. And the International Monetary Fund predicts that Canada will be the fastest-growing economy of the G-7 countries during the 1990s, and will keep a tighter rein on inflation than any other G-7 country but Japan.

A Trading Nation   Canada is a trading nation. Three-quarters of its exports go to the United States, the world's largest importer-exporter. The U.S., in turn, supplies almost three-quarters of Canada's imports. In fact, Canada and the U.S. are the world's largest bilateral trading partners. Canada's trade with the U.S. in 1989 amounted to U.S.$171 billion, well ahead of U.S. trade with Japan, worth U.S.$137 billion. Canada's other major trading partners are the United Kingdom, Germany and South Korea.

OECD

- **high level of per capita income**
- **low rate of population increase**
- **industrial sector in which large-scale corporate activity has steadily increased**
- **work force with high levels of education and training**
- **rapidly expanding service sector**
- **government sector that has expanded rapidly in the 20th century, both in size and in range of economic functions**

Developing Countries

- **low level of per capita income**
- **rapid rate of population increase**
- **majority of population engaged in low-productivity agriculture**
- **work force with low levels of education and training**
- **dependence on a few primary commodity exports**

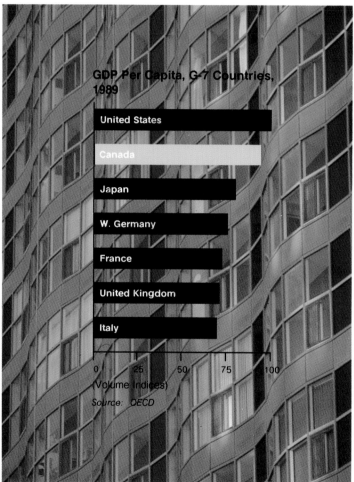

GDP Per Capita, G-7 Countries, 1989

United States

Canada

Japan

W. Germany

France

United Kingdom

Italy

0   25   50   75   100

(Volume Indices)

Source: OECD

Like most European OECD countries, Canada exports about 30% of its goods and services. Canada's exports have grown by about 10% a year during the last 10 years, slightly faster than the global average.

Industry   Industry has traditionally been Canada's engine of trade and economic growth, and Canadian-made end products in 1990 comprised 47% of total merchandise exports, up from 32% in 1980.

Canada is the world's largest exporter of railway rolling stock and equipment – with about 21% of the export market – and the world's third-largest exporter of automobiles after Japan and Germany. Canada is also among the world's top five exporters of aircraft and parts, and is the United States' single largest source of imported railway and aircraft equipment.

One of Canada's major exports is expertise. Canadian specialists in engineering, mining, geology, biotechnology, aerial surveying, computer software, electronics and manufacturing work all over the globe, on projects ranging from telecommunications to nuclear power stations.

Many Canadians volunteer their services through the Canadian Executive Service Organization (CESO), a private, non-profit corporation that supplies professional and technical knowledge to organizations in developing countries. CESO has nearly 3,000 experienced Canadian women and men, each of whom works abroad on projects lasting about two to three months.

Canada is the World's . . .
Canada is the world's largest producer of zinc and uranium, and the second-largest producer of cobalt, gypsum, potash, nickel, asbestos and titanium concentrates. About 80% of

Turn on the Canada
Canadian rivers generate 15% of the world's hydroelectric power, and nearly two-thirds of Canada's total electricity.

Canada's mineral production is exported, mostly to the United States, Japan and Western Europe. Canada also leads the world in exports of forestry products, including about 30% of the world's pulp and almost 60% of its newsprint.

Canada ranks fifth in the world in electrical generating capacity, and second in nuclear electricity generating capacity.

Natural Resources   Canadians have traditionally been portrayed as "hewers of wood and drawers of water" because of their dependence on natural resources as a staple of trade. There is still some truth to this, although today Canadians are increasingly aware of the risk of relying too much on exports of natural resources – especially non-renewable ones.

Yet natural resource products still account for more than 40% of Canada's exports – one of the highest proportions of any industrialized nation.

Energy   Energy is Canada's second-most important export after automobiles, and accounts for roughly 10% of the nation's exports and 4% of world energy production. Among OECD countries, only the United States ranks higher.

Canada's major energy export, by value, is heavy crude oil, 90% of which is sold to the United States. About half of all Western Canadian coal production is exported to Japanese steelmakers.

Canada's Investment Boom   Canada is experiencing the biggest wave of foreign investment in its history. There has always been a great deal of foreign direct investment in Canada, particularly by U.S.-based multinationals. Today, the majority of foreign investment takes the form of bonds that require fixed interest payments. The proportion of Canadian bonds purchased by foreign investors grew from 29% in 1970 to about 50% in 1990. Foreign investors in 1990 held 38% of all Government of Canada bonds. Half of these bonds were held by Japanese interests.

Canadian firms are responding to global economic integration by investing abroad. In 1960, Canadian investment abroad was about 20% of foreign investment in Canada – by 1988, it was more than 50%.

Almost 90% of Canadian investment abroad is in developed countries, two-thirds of this in the United States. Canadian firms tend to concentrate their investments in companies in the same industry, notably manufacturing, mining and finance. Canadian manufacturers account for about 50% of investments abroad, followed by the financial and merchandising industries.

Canada Competes   Some of Canada's greatest achievements during the past 100 years have been in communications – from the invention of the telephone to the world's first domestic communications satellite, the Anik A-1, launched in 1972. Telecommunications equipment exports have increased by about 10% a year during the last 10 years.

Canadians are also leaders in space sciences and technology, and have been for more than 25 years. Canada was the third country to enter the satellite age with the 1962 launch of the Alouette satellite, and the Canadarm remote manipulator was a vital component of recent U.S. space shuttles.

Canada is also an international leader in nuclear power technology. The CANDU (CANadian Deuterium Uranium) reactor system is considered by many to be the world's most efficient, and the CANDU station at Pickering, Ontario, is the largest producer of commercial nuclear power in the world.

Canada Calling

In 1988-89, Canada had 780 telephones per 1,000 people according to the UN's *Human Development Report 1992*. This is twice the number of Spain, more than three times that of Portugal and almost nine times that of the former Soviet Union. Only Switzerland, Denmark, Sweden and the U.S. ranked higher than Canada.

Food for the World

Canada has long been one of the world's most generous suppliers of food aid – mostly shipments of wheat, flour and canola oil. In 1988-89, Canadian food aid shipments of $431.5 million were the highest in the world. Canada shipped this food to needy countries using multilateral agencies such as the Red Cross and the United Nations.

Canadian firms are world leaders in remote sensing, geophysical exploration, medicine and bioengineering. Canadian breakthroughs in laser surgery, organ transplants and genetic crop and livestock improvements are now commonplace.

Canada Snapshots

The United Nations has studied some 160 countries, ranking them according to life expectancy, education and income – using more than 40 indicators of human development – and determined that Canada is the best place to live in the world. Here is how some of the other top industrialized countries rank: Japan is 2nd, the United States is 6th, France 8th, the United Kingdom 10th, Germany 12th and Italy 21st.

An Apple a Day . . . The UN's *Human Development Report 1992* compares countries in terms of health, wealth and more. (For some topics, the data are not always for the same years; in these cases, a range of years is given, for example, 1985-89). The report finds that average life expectancy in Canada is 77 years, 12 years longer than the world average and slightly shorter than the world's longest – 78.6 years (Japan). And yet more than half of Canadians will die of circulatory and respiratory diseases, most of them linked to sedentary lifestyles, fat-rich diets, cigarette smoking and alcohol consumption. About three in 10 Canadians smoke cigarettes, for example, compared with roughly two in 10 Greeks (lowest) and more than five in 10 Danes (highest).

In total health expenditure as a percentage of GDP, Canada ties for third place with France at 8.6%, behind the United States at 11.2% and Sweden at 9%. Most industrial countries spend 8.3% of GDP on health care.

Work, Wages and Wealth   Canada has one of the world's widest income gaps between rich and poor. Although this gap is narrower than in the United States, it is nearly twice as wide as in other countries of the industrialized world such as Japan and Belgium. Some other findings from the *Human Development Report 1992*:

- Canada's labour force made up 50.3% of its population in 1988-90, placing Canada ninth behind Australia, whose workers comprised 63.8% of its population. The industrial world average was 48.8%.
- Canada's unemployment rate in 1990 was 8.1% – higher than the industrial world average of 6.4% and 7th highest in that category after Spain (15.9%), Ireland (14.0%), Poland (10.4%), Italy (9.9%), Denmark (9.6%) and France (9.0%). Lowest was Switzerland with 0.6%. By early 1992, Canada's unemployment rate had risen above 11%.

Dollars Into Sense   Investing money in education is important to Canadians, as evidenced by the fact that Canadians on average have had more years of schooling than citizens of any other nation except the United States. Canadians receive 12.1 years of schooling, two more years than the industrial world average and three times the developing world average.

Canadians in the Lab
According to the UN's *Human Development Report 1992*, Canada had 177 scientists and technicians per 1,000 people in 1985-89, more than twice the industrial world average and more than eight times the world average. Sweden was highest with 262; the United States was near the bottom with 55.

Welcome to Canada
Canada's record in welcoming international refugees – when the size of our population is taken into account – is second to none. This outstanding humanitarian tradition was recognized in 1986 when the United Nations High Commissioner for Refugees presented the Nansen Medal to the people of Canada. This was the first time in the medal's 40-year history that it had ever been awarded to an entire nation.

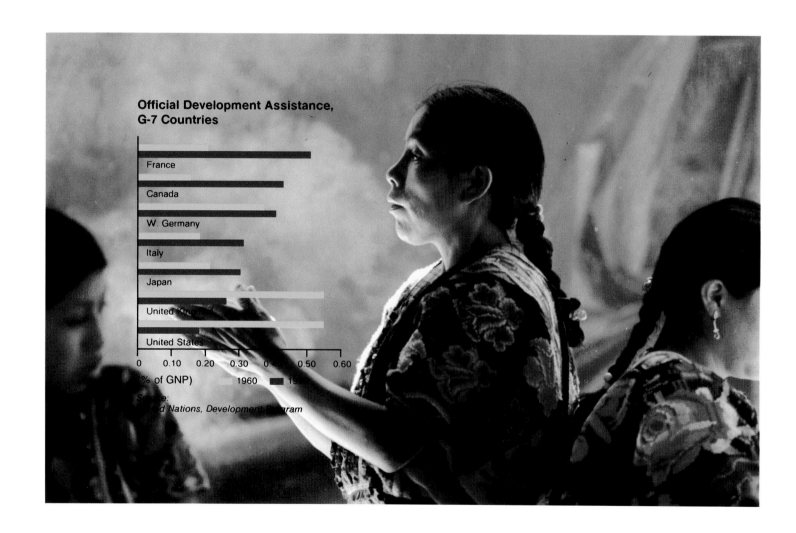

Official Development Assistance,
G-7 Countries

France

Canada

W. Germany

Italy

Japan

United Ki...

United States

0   0.10   0.20   0.30   ...   0.50   0.60

(% of GNP)   1960   19...

Source:
...d Nations, Development Program

Americans receive 12.3 years of education. Canada's total education expenditure as a percentage of GDP in 1986 was 7.2%, placing Canada third-highest in the world after Sweden and Denmark and above the industrial world average of 5.9%.

Women in Canada, Women in the World   Sexual inequality in the Canadian workplace has been reduced – but it still exists:

- Canadian women get paid more than their counterparts in the United States and Japan, but that isn't saying much – American and Japanese women are the lowest paid relative to men in the industrialized world. In 1986, Japanese women were paid 50% of men's wages, American women received 59%, and Canadian women got 63%. This compared with highs of 89% in Sweden, 88% in Australia and Iceland, and 85% in Norway.

- Only one in nine Canadian members of Parliament were women in 1990. In comparison, in Sweden and Finland six out of 10 were women; in Japan, two out of 100 were women.

- Women comprised 44.3% of Canada's work force (above the industrial world average of 43.7%) in 1990. The highest was the former Soviet Union at 48.3% and the lowest was Malta at 25.1%.

Hooked on Media   Every day, the world publishes some 1,000 books. Every eight years, the global store of knowledge doubles. It's been said that a big city newspaper may contain more information than the average person living in 17th century England might have encountered in a lifetime. Clearly, we are living in the "information age":

- The developing world had 51 television sets per 1,000 people in 1988-89, and the world as a whole had 153 – Canada had 626. This placed Canada second after the United States (814) and ahead of Japan (610), and considerably higher than the industrial world average of 493.

- Canadians attended the cinema about three times a year in 1987-89, which was almost three times more often than people from the Netherlands (1.1 times), although far less often than people from Romania – they attended about 8.8 times a year. The industrial world average was 2.9 visits.

- Canadian libraries held 5.6 library books per person in 1986-88, fewer than the industrial world average (6.0). Sweden led with 12.9, Canada placed 15th, and Italy trailed in 33rd place with 0.6 books.

- Daily newspaper circulation per 1,000 people in the developing world was 43 in 1988-89, in the industrial world it was 337, and in Canada it was 231. Japan led the industrial world with 566; Portugal was last with 41.

The Cost of Affluence   High levels of income – of the kind enjoyed by many Canadians – are no guarantee against human deprivation. The UN's *Human Development Report 1992* says there is considerable human distress in rich societies. Here are some of the report's findings on Canada:

- Canada's murder rate in 1987-88 was low at 2.1 per 100,000 – exactly half the industrial world average and considerably less than the world's highest: the United States with nine per 100,000.

Japan and Ireland had a murder rate of 0.8, the lowest among industrialized countries.

- In 1980-85, some 30 Canadian women in 100,000 aged 15 to 59 reported being raped. This was fewer than the industrialized world average of 48, but still placed Canada 5th highest among the industrial nations after the United States (114), the Netherlands (92), Finland (40) and Sweden (34).
- Hungary led the world in suicides in 1988, with 45.8 per 100,000, almost triple the industrial world average of 16. Japan placed 9th (19.7), Canada and Iceland were 14th (14.6), the United States was 17th (13.0).

Canada in the World Community

In bilingual, democratic, multicultural Canada, where someone might sing in French, work in English but dream in Vietnamese, adapting to world events – even compromising – has always been necessary. And Canadians in the world community, whether discussing trade or immigration, disarmament or food aid, have earned a reputation for cordiality, tolerance and understanding. Canada has been working to make the world a safer and better place for more than 40 years. Canada is the seventh-largest aid donor in the western world, with Canadians contributing the equivalent of $100 per person – or about one-half of 1% of Canada's GDP – in assistance to developing countries every year.

All Canadian aid is given as grants and contributions – not loans – and supports the development efforts of some 85 international organizations, including UN agencies, humanitarian institutions, and development banks. The Canadian International Development Agency (CIDA) supports more than 400 non-governmental organizations and institutions, including churches, service clubs, co-operatives, unions and universities. Every year, CIDA supports about 1,000 government-to-government projects and about 6,500 non-governmental organization projects. These range from digging wells to providing basic health care, from fostering joint ventures between businesses to educating Third World students in Canada.

Canada was a founding member of the United Nations in 1945, and has always placed great importance on supporting the UN system. Canada has served at regular intervals on the UN's Economic and Social Council, and is currently serving on the UN Security Council at a time when the UN's function in international affairs is being revitalized.

As well as being the fourth-largest contributor to the UN's budget, Canada makes voluntary contributions to many UN programs, including the development program, the high commission for refugees, the children's fund, and the world food program.

Canada is a member of the Commonwealth, a unique community of 48 sovereign nations, associated states and dependent territories that covers one-quarter of the globe and comprises

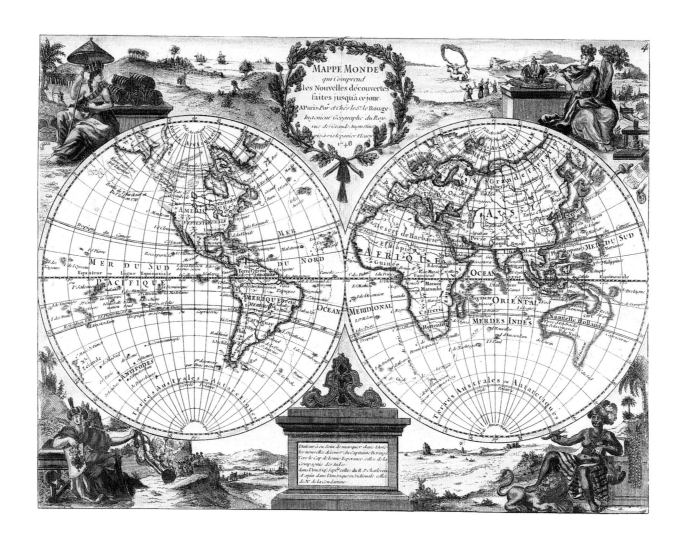

more than a fifth of its inhabitants. The Commonwealth includes developed and developing countries that share many traditions, attitudes, political and social values, and institutions. Canada works with the Commonwealth's 250 non-governmental organizations to foster common values.

Canada's participation in la Francophonie is the natural extension in international affairs of Canadian bilingualism. ''La Francophonie'' is the term given to the community of countries sharing the French language and culture. Like the Commonwealth, la Francophonie has evolved into a forum for international problem solving. It also gives French culture in Canada an international dimension.

As a trading power, Canada has particular interest in economic co-operation and the growth and stability of the world economy. The increasing interdependence of national economies has resulted in a series of economic summits that bring together the leaders of the G-7, including Canada. Canada is co-operating with these countries in defining and addressing the specific problems of the world economy. Canada also influences global monetary reform negotiations through its contributions to the International Monetary Fund and the World Bank.

Canada has 115 independent diplomatic and consular missions in 82 countries, and maintains diplomatic relations with 84 others. More than 100 countries have diplomatic missions in Canada's capital, Ottawa, and another 48 countries have non-resident accreditation.

Canada is a partner with the United States in the North American Aerospace Defence Command (NORAD), through which it participates in aerospace surveillance and warning, air defence, and other measures.

Along with the United States and many Western European countries, Canada was one of the original signatories of the North Atlantic Treaty Organization (NATO) in 1949. Through NATO, Canada contributes to the defence of Europe while fostering political, economic and scientific relations.

PHOTOGRAPHIC CREDITS

Page 2
Lake Superior, Ontario.
Richard Hartmier/First Light

Page 6
Tom Van Sant/Geosphere Project/1990

Page 8
Donald Standfield/First Light

Page 12
George Hunter

Page 14
Darwin Wiggett/First Light

Page 16
George Hunter

Page 18
Northwest Territories.
Stephane Poulain/FourByFive

Page 20
Mike Beedell/Miller Comstock

Page 22
E. Otto/Miller Comstock

Page 24
Scott Leslie/First Light

Page 26
Winnipeg, Manitoba.
O. Bierwagen/Miller Comstock

Page 28
W. Greibeling/Miller Comstock

Page 30
Tree in Field.
Stephen Livick/Canadian Museum of Contemporary
Photography (CMCP) Collection

Page 32
La Rivière, Manitoba.
Derek Trask/SuperStock

Page 36
Immigrants, Quebec, about 1911.
William James Topley/National Archives of
Canada/PA 10265

Page 38
Roy Luckow/Image Finders

Page 40
Elderly couple, community hall.
R. Michael Stuckey/Miller Comstock

Page 44
E. Otto/Miller Comstock

Page 46
Robert Semeniuk/First Light

Page 48
Clara Gutsche/Canada Council Art Bank

Page 50
Barb & Ron Kroll/Miller Comstock

Page 52
W. Greibeling/Miller Comstock

Page 54
Mennonite Meeting House, two children.
Norman Lightfoot/Miller Comstock

Page 56
Cape Breton Island, Nova Scotia.
George Hunter

Page 60
Dawn Goss/First Light

Page 62
George Hunter

Page 64
Communication dish.
Steve Vidler/Miller Comstock

Page 68
CN Tower, Toronto: Ron Watts/First Light
Lion's Gate Bridge, Vancouver:
Dave Watters/First Light

Page 74
Child, desk, forest.
Thomas Bruckbauer/Image Finders

Page 80
From ''Serie: *Affichage et automobile, Valleyfield P.Q., 1976*'' Serge Clément

Page 82
Early women's hockey team.
National Archives of Canada/PA 74583

Page 86
Allen McInnis/First Light

Page 88
François-Xavier Borel Fonds/National Archives of
Canada/C-130681

Page 94
Henry Georgi/Miller Comstock

Page 96
National Arts Centre Orchestra, Ottawa.
Cattroll-Ritcey Photo

Page 98
Malak

Page 100
Royal Winnipeg Ballet.
Todd Korol/First Light

Page 104
Steve Short/First Light

Page 106
Henry Georgi/Miller Comstock

Page 108
Toronto Dance Theatre.
Cylla von Tiedemann

Page 132
Great Regina Plain.
George Hunter

Page 136
attr. to Henri Beau/National Archives of Canada/C 17059

Page 138
Ron Watts/First Light

Page 140
Vancouver Harbour.
Fred Herzog/First Light

Page 144
Robert W. Allen/First Light

Page 146
K. Sommerer/Miller Comstock

Page 148
Silicon wafers: Hans Blohm/Masterfile
Conveyor and biscuits: George Hunter

Page 150
George Hunter

Page 152
Danny Eigenmann/Reflexion

Page 156
"Any Old Thing No. 7"
(Black and white diffraction image, city steps)
Lawrence Weissmann

Page 158
A Caribou, the Yukon.
Thomas Kitchin/Image Finders

Page 162
Downtown Toronto: Benjamin Rondel/First Light
Building abstract, Toronto: Brian Milne/First Light

Page 164
George Hunter

Page 168
Tenango, Guatemala.
A.E. Sirulnikoff/First Light

Page 170
Deryk Bodington

Page 172
map author: Georg Louis le Rouge/National Archives of
Canada/NMC 8276

Page 174
*"Arthur Worthington and Jack Peterson, Victoria Day
Parade, Victoria, British Columbia"* Nina
Raginsky/Canadian Museum of Contemporary
Photography (CMCP) Collection

IBLIOGRAPHY

S E L E C T E D　　　S O U R C E S

Chapter 1

Bantam. *The Bantam Illustrated World Atlas*. New York: Bantam Books, 1989.

Beck, Emily Morison, Ed. *Bartlett's Familiar Quotations, Fourteenth Edition*. Toronto: Little, Brown and Co., 1968.

Environment Canada. *Climates of Canada*. Cat. No. En56-1/1990. Ottawa: Minister of Supply and Services, 1990.

Chapter 2

Statistics Canada:

Canada's North, A Profile	Cat. No. 98-122
Focus on Canada: Canada's Seniors	Cat. No. 98-121
Focus on Canada: Canada's Population from Ocean to Ocean	Cat. No. 98-120
Current Demographic Analysis: Income of Immigrants in Canada	Cat. No. 91-527
Focus on Canada: Canada, a Linguistic Profile	Cat. No. 98-131
Focus on Canada: Women and the Labour Force	Cat. No. 98-125

Statistics Canada/Canadian Centre for Health Information. "Births 1989". *Health Reports*. Cat. No. 82-003 (Quarterly) 1991.

Employment and Immigration Canada. *Immigration to Canada: Economic Impacts*. 1989.

Employment and Immigration Canada. *Immigration to Canada; Issues for Discussion*. 1989.

Health and Welfare Canada. *Charting Canada's Future*. 1990.

Health and Welfare Canada. *Canada's Seniors; A Dynamic Force*. (Cat. No. H88-3/1-1988). 1990.

Indian and Northern Affairs Canada. *Highlights of Aboriginal Conditions, 1981-2001; Part I, Demographic Trends*. 1990.

Indian and Northern Affairs Canada. *Highlights of Aboriginal Conditions, 1981-2001; Part II, Social Conditions*. 1990.

Indian and Northern Affairs Canada. *Indians and Inuit of Canada*. 1990.

Chapter 3

Statistics Canada:

Adult Literacy in Canada	Cat. No. 89-525
Cable Television	Cat. No. 56-205
Canadian Crime Statistics	Cat. No. 85-205
Communications	Cat. No. 56-001
Household Facilities and Equipment	Cat. No. 64-202
Policing in Canada	Cat. No. 85-523

Radio and Television Broadcasting	Cat. No. 56-204
Telecommunications Statistics	Cat. No. 56-201
Television Viewing	Cat. No. 87-208

Association of Canadian Universities and Colleges of Canada. *Trends: The Canadian University in Profile – 1991 Edition.* Ottawa: Association of Universities and Colleges of Canada, 1991.

Beaudoin, Senator Gerald, and Dobbie, Dorothy, M.P., joint chairmen. *A Renewed Canada: The Report of the Special Joint Committee of the Senate and the House of Commons.* Ottawa: Minister of Supply and Services, 1992.

Canadian Radio-television and Telecommunications Commission *CRTC: The Year in Review 1990-1991* (Cat. No. BC-91-1991). 1991.

Communications Canada. *Canadian Telecommunications – an overview of the Canadian Telecommunications Carriage Industry* (Cat. No. Co22-44/1988).

Communications Canada. *Canadian Voices Canadian Choices: A New Broadcasting Policy for Canada* (Cat. No. Co22-82/1988).

Communications Canada. *Communications for the Twenty-First Century: Media and Messages in the Information Age.* (Cat. No. Co22-78/1987).

United Nations Educational, Scientific and Cultural Organization. *UNESCO World Education Report, 1991.* Paris: United Nations Educational, Scientific and Cultural Organization, 1991.

Chapter 4

Statistics Canada. Current culture statistics publications:

Book Publishing	Cat. No. 87-210
Performing Arts	Cat. No. 87-209
Television Viewing	Cat. No. 87-208
Heritage Institutions	Cat. No. 87-207
Government Expenditures on Culture	Cat. No. 87-206
Film and Video	Cat. No. 87-204
Periodical Publishing	Cat. No. 87-203
Sound Recording	Cat. No. 87-202

Statistics Canada. Culture Statistics Division. Unpublished data, 1992.

Statistics Canada. *Focus on Culture.* (Cat. No. 87-004). Vols 1-4.

Communications Canada. *Vital Links: Canadian Cultural Industries.* 1987.

Heritage Canada. *Annual Report 1990-91.* Ottawa: Heritage Canada, 1991.

S E L E C T E D   S O U R C E S

Chapter 5

Statistics Canada

Canadian Economic Observer	Cat. No. 11-010
Canadian Economic Observer Historical Statistical Supplement	Cat. No. 11-210
Perspectives on Labour and Income	Cat. No. 75-001
Canada's International Investment Position	Cat. No. 67-202

Statistics Canada. *CANSIM (CANSIM, Statistics Canada's public electronic database, is a comprehensive source of Canadian economic data. Information on gaining access is available at Statistics Canada's Regional Reference Centres, listed in the back pages of this book).*

Cross, Philip, (Economist, Statistics Canada). Unpublished paper on Canada's current economic conditions. 1992.

Organization for Economic Cooperation and Development. *OECD Economic Surveys: Canada.* Paris: Organization for Economic Cooperation and Development, 1991.

Chapter 6

Statistics Canada. *Assessing Canada's Position in World Trade:* *The Statistical Dimension.* Ottawa: World Trade Data Base, Tiers, 1989.

Cross, Philip. (Economist, Statistics Canada) "Canada in the World," unpublished paper. 1992.

External Affairs and International Trade Canada. *Canada: An Overview.* Ottawa: Secretary of State for External Affairs. 1990.

External Affairs and International Trade Canada. *Facts Canada.* (Information package) External Affairs and International Trade Canada. undated.

Immigration and Refugee Board. Backgrounder: *Immigration and Refugee Board.* (discussion paper) Ottawa, 1992.

Litchfield, Patrick. "The Contrarian Case for Canada," *Canadian Business,* Toronto: December 1991.

Malcom, Andrew. "Northern Contradiction." *Saturday Night Magazine,* Toronto: December 1987.

United Nations. *The United Nations Human Development Report 1992.* New York: Oxford University Press, 1992.

Wurman, Richard Saul. *Information Anxiety.* New York: Doubleday, 1989.

SELECTED SOURCES

Common Sources:

Statistics Canada. *The Canada Year Book*. Cat. No. 11-402

Statistics Canada. *Canada: A Portrait, 53rd Edition*. Cat. No. 11-403

Statistics Canada. *Canadian Social Trends*. Cat. No. 11-008 Monthly.

Colombo, John Robert, Ed. *Colombo's Canadian Quotations*. Edmonton: Hurtig, 1974.

Colombo, John Robert. *Columbo's New Canadian Quotations*. Edmonton: Hurtig, 1987.

Colombo, John Robert, Ed. *The Dictionary of Canadian Quotations*. Toronto: Stoddart, 1991.

Colombo, John Robert. *The Canadian Global Almanac*. Toronto: Global Press, 1991.

Marsh, James, Ed. *The Canadian Encyclopedia, Second Edition*. Edmonton: Hurtig, 1988.

Other Sources:

Selected quotations were printed with permission from McClelland and Stewart Limited, Stoddart Publishing Co. Limited, MacMillan of Canada, Simon & Pierre, McGraw-Hill Book Company and the Ottawa Citizen.

Publications, interviews and/or unpublished material:
Canadian Government:
    Statistics Canada
    Canada Council
    Canada Post
    Canadian Broadcasting Corporation
    Canadian Radio-television and Telecommunications Commission
    Communications Canada
    Environment Canada
    External Affairs and International Trade Canada
    Health and Welfare Canada

Other organizations:
    American Federation of Musicians of Canada and the United States
    Association of Universities and Colleges of Canada
    The Foundation for Economic Education
    The Organization for Economic Cooperation and Development (OECD)
    The United Nations
    The United Nations Educational, Scientific and Cultural Organization (UNESCO)

STATISTICS CANADA

REGIONAL REFERENCE CENTRES

Newfoundland and Labrador

Hugh Ridler
1-709-772-0137

Advisory Services
Statistics Canada
3rd Floor
Viking Building
Crosbie Road
St. John's, Newfoundland
A1B 3P2

Local calls:	(709) 772-4073
Toll free service:	1-800-563-4255
Fax number:	(709) 772-6433

Maritime Provinces

Andrew Maw
1-902-426-6374

Advisory Services
Statistics Canada
North American Life Centre

3rd Floor
1770 Market Street
Halifax, Nova Scotia
B3J 3M3

Local calls:	(902) 426-5331
Toll free service:	1-800-565-7192
Fax number:	(902) 426-9538

Quebec

Yvan Deslauriers
1-514-283-5742

Advisory Services
Statistics Canada
200 René Lévesque Blvd. W
Guy Favreau Complex
Suite 412, East Tower
Montreal, Quebec
H2Z 1X4

Local calls:	(514) 283-5725
Toll free service:	1-800-361-2831
Fax number:	(514) 283-9350

REGIONAL REFERENCE CENTRES

National Capital Region

Hélène Lavoie
1-613-951-8198

Statistical Reference Centre (NCR)
Statistics Canada
R.H. Coats Bldg., Lobby
Holland Avenue
Ottawa, Ontario
K1A 0T6

Local calls: (613) 951-8116
If outside the local calling area, please
dial the toll free number for your province.
Fax number: (613) 951-0581

Ontario

Gregg Connolly
1-416-973-6257

Advisory Services
Statistics Canada
10th Floor

Arthur Meighen Building
25 St. Clair Avenue East
Toronto, Ontario
M4T 1M4

Local calls: (416) 973-6586
Toll free service: 1-800-263-1136
Fax number: (416) 973-7475

Manitoba

Bernie Gloyn
1-204-983-3257

Advisory Services
Statistics Canada
Suite 300
MacDonald Building
344 Edmonton Street
Winnipeg, Manitoba
R3B 3L9

Local calls: (204) 983-4020
Toll free service: 1-800-542-3404
Fax number: (204) 983-7543

REGIONAL REFERENCE CENTRES

Saskatchewan

Larry Deters
1-306-780-5404

Advisory Services
Statistics Canada
Avord Tower, 9th Floor
2002 Victoria Avenue
Regina, Saskatchewan
S4P 0R7

Local calls:	(306) 780-5405
Toll free service:	1-800-667-7164
Fax number:	(306) 780-5403

Alberta and the Northwest Territories

Bruce Meyers
1-403-495-4659

Advisory Services
Statistics Canada
8th Floor
Park Square
10001 Bellamy Hill
Edmonton, Alberta
T5J 3B6

Local calls:	(403) 495-3027
Toll free service:	1-800-282-3907
N.W.T. – Call collect:	1-403-495-3028
Fax number:	(403) 495-5318

REGIONAL REFERENCE CENTRES

Southern Alberta

Jacques Ouellet
1-403-292-6719

Advisory Services
Statistics Canada
First Street Plaza
Room 401
138 – 4th Avenue South East
Calgary, Alberta
T2G 4Z6

Local calls:	(403) 292-6717
Toll free service:	1-800-472-9708
Fax number:	(403) 292-4958

British Columbia and the Yukon

Norry Fitzpatrick
1-604-666-2931

Advisory Services
Statistics Canada
Sinclair Centre
757 West Hastings Street
Suite 440F
Vancouver, B.C.
V6C 3C9

Local calls:	(604) 666-3691
Toll free service:	1-800-663-1551
	(except Atlin, B.C.)
Yukon and Atlin, B.C.	Zenith 08913
Fax number:	(604) 666-4863

$\mathcal{I}$NDEX

Aboriginal languages   41-42

Aboriginal peoples   10, 11, 13, 15, 41-42, 45, 47, 49, 59, 91, 92, 123

Ackerman, Marianne   85

Adams, Bryan   103

Aerospace   134, 173

Aging of Canada's population   39-41, 77-78

Aircraft and parts   141, 163

Alberta   9, 11, 15, 17, 42, 43, 53, 69, 75, 135, 149

Alcohol consumption   77, 166

Amateur sport   107

American Federation of Musicians of the United States and Canada   89

Anne of Green Gables   92, 93

Appalachians   4, 9, 10

Arctic   5, 7, 13, 23

Arts   13, 71, 84-92, 93, 99, 101, 102, 103, 105, 121, 125, 127, 129, 130

Athletes   107

Atlantic Region   19, 27

Atwood, Margaret   92

Australia   35, 101, 167, 169

Automobiles   149, 154, 163, 165

Automotive products   141

Baby-boom generation   37, 39, 41, 75, 76

Baffin Island   7, 13, 125

Bank Act   145

Bank rate   145

Banking system   139

Beam, Carl   110, 123

Béliveau, Jean   83

Bell, John Kim   92

Benoit, Claude-Phillipe   119

Bering Strait   10

Bicycling   105

Bilingualism   41, 43, 49, 51, 173

Bioengineering   141, 166

Blackburn, Frederick   107

Blackfoot Indians   15

Blended families   34, 39

Bond, Eleanor   110, 115

Bondar, Roberta   133

Bonds   139, 147, 165

Bonds, Government of Canada   147, 165

Books   92, 93, 95, 169

Boreal forest   4, 9, 17

Bourgeois, Lorène   121

Brasseur, Isabelle   107

Brazil   41, 139, 160

British Columbia   4, 7, 9, 11, 13, 15, 17, 19, 23, 41, 42, 43, 53, 69, 91, 135, 149

Broadcasting   70, 71, 101, 102, 103, 105

Business   134, 137, 151, 155

Business cycle   143

Business investment   137, 147, 165

Cabinet   61

Calgary Eye Opener   76

Campbell's Survey on Well-Being in Canada   105

Canada Council   87, 89, 90

Canada Post   70, 97, 135

Canada-U.S. Free Trade Agreement   137, 142, 147

Canada-U.S. trade   141

Canadian Broadcasting Corporation   71, 89, 99, 101, 102

Canadian Executive Service Organization   163

Canadian International Development Agency   171

Canadian Radio-television and Telecommunications Commission   71, 101-105

Canadian Shield   4, 9, 19

Canadian War Museum   91

Canadian-content   84, 99, 101, 105

CANDU reactor   165

Capital formation   137

Cardinal, Douglas   3, 91

Cellular phone   69

Central Canada 25, 119, 147, 149

Changing residence 43

Charter of Rights and Freedoms 61

Chartered banks 137, 139,145

Child tax credit 79

China 17, 160

Clark, Joe 58

Climate 21-27, 53, 70

Coast Mountains 25

Cockburn, Bruce 103

Cohen, Dian 72

Colgrass, Ulla 89

Colleges 67, 73, 76, 87, 145

Common-law families 34, 39, 47, 49, 51

Commonwealth, the 171-173

Communications 58, 67-73, 79, 84, 155, 165

Communications Canada 71, 72, 105

Communications satellites 70, 72, 160

Compact discs 89

Computers 69, 72, 73, 137, 141, 163

Connors, Stompin' Tom 103

Constitution Act 58-61

Constitution, the 45, 58-65, 76

Consumer and Corporate Affairs Canada 135

Consumer spending 154

Consumers 29, 93, 103, 134-143, 153, 154

Cordillera Indians 13

Courts 61-67, 154

Creates, Marlene 111, 125

Cree Indians 15, 42, 45, 84

Criminal Code 66

Crown corporations 61, 70, 87, 99, 135, 155

Currency 139, 141, 142, 145, 147

Cutrone, Angela 107

Czechoslovakia 41

Dafoe, John, W. 59

Daigle, Sylvie 107

Daignault, Michel 107

Dance 45, 84, 85, 87, 89

Debt, government 134

Decline in Canada's population 34

Defence 65, 154, 155, 173

Deficit 134, 141, 155

Dene 11

Dion, Celine 103

Distinct society 58

Divorce 37, 39, 51, 53

Double-income families 34, 37

Drumheller, Alberta 90

Eastern Woodlands Indians 17, 19

Economic growth 137, 142, 143, 147, 163

Economy, the 35, 37, 73, 78, 87, 134-155, 160, 161, 165, 173

Education 35, 39, 58, 59, 63, 65, 73-77, 135, 137, 151, 154, 161, 166, 167, 169

Edwards, Bob 76

Eisler, Lloyd 107

Employment and Immigration Canada 135

Energy 29, 155, 160, 165

English (the language) 34, 41, 43, 47, 49, 51, 53, 58, 71, 75, 95, 97, 99, 102, 171

European Economic Community 17, 142, 153

Exercise 77, 105, 107

Expenditure, government 154

Exports 21, 95, 97, 139-143, 149, 151, 161, 163, 165

External Affairs and International Trade Canada 71, 113

Falk, Gathie 110, 127

Families 34, 37, 39, 47, 49, 51, 79, 153

Family allowance 79, 135, 154, 155

Federal Court 66

Federal government 29, 58, 61-65, 67, 70, 78, 84, 95, 97, 101, 105, 107, 135-139, 147, 155

Fertility 34, 37, 47, 49, 51, 53

Fibre optics 69, 72, 73

Film 84, 97, 99, 101

Finance 139, 165

Financial institutions 137, 139

Financial sector 137

Food aid 166, 171

Foreign ownership 95, 137

Forest industry 13, 17, 19, 21, 147, 149, 163

Forsey, Eugene 59, 63

Foundation to Assist Canadian Talent on Record 105

France 35, 41, 65, 73, 95, 103, 141, 142, 143, 145, 160, 161, 166, 167

French (the language) 34, 41, 43, 47, 49, 51, 53, 58, 71, 75, 95, 97, 99, 102, 171, 173

Fresh water 9

Fulford, Robert 84

G-7 nations 73, 79, 161, 173

Gagnon, Sylvain 107

Gardening 77, 105

General Agreement on Tariffs and Trade 78, 142

Geophysical exploration 141, 166

Germany 41, 73, 141, 142, 143, 154, 160, 161, 163, 166

Globalization 70, 78, 84, 95

Goods and Services Tax 95, 97, 155

Goodwin, Betty 111, 113

Government 27, 35, 58-66, 70, 72, 73, 77, 79, 84, 95, 99, 105, 135, 137, 145, 153, 154, 155, 160, 161

Governor General 61, 63

Great Britain 61, 63, 101

Great Lakes 19, 25, 27

Great Lakes-St. Lawrence Lowlands 4, 9, 17

Great Lakes-St. Lawrence Seaway 9, 17

Great Plains 4, 7

Great Slave Lake 13, 134

Gross Domestic Product 73, 75, 76, 79, 84, 134, 135-139, 142, 143, 149, 151, 153, 155, 161, 167, 169, 171

Gross National Product 79

Guaranteed Income Supplement 79

Haida Indians 13, 42

Halifax 23, 134

Health and Welfare Canada 77, 79

Health care 39, 41, 58, 78, 79, 135, 137, 153, 154, 167, 171

Heritage 11, 90, 91

Heritage Canada 91

High Arctic Islands 13

High technology 72

Highway, Tomson 45, 92, 159

House of Commons 61-65, 71

Hudson Bay 5, 9

Hydroelectric power 13, 19, 21, 163

Ice Age 4, 7, 10

Immigration 10, 11, 34-37, 43, 45, 49-53, 65, 75, 78, 92, 160

Imports 95, 141, 142, 161

Income security 79

Income tax 155

Incomes 35, 37, 137, 143, 153

Industry, Science and Technology Canada 135

Inflation 135, 142-147, 161

Information 67-72, 169

Information Age 69, 169

Information Society 71

Information technology 72

Infrastructure 58, 75-78, 135

Integrated Services Digital Network 73

Interest rates 137, 139, 143, 145, 147

International Monetary Fund 161, 173

Interpol 67

Inuktitut 42

Investment 78, 99, 137, 139, 145, 147, 160, 165

Italy 73, 142, 143, 160, 161, 166, 167, 169

Japan 13, 17, 73, 85, 92, 93, 141, 142, 143, 153,

154, 160, 161, 163, 166, 167, 169, 171

Juno Awards 103

Kennedy, John, F. 141

King, Alan 134

Koop, Wanda 129

La Francophonie 173

La La La Human Steps 87

Labour force 39, 69, 76, 135, 137, 143, 145, 153, 167

Lambert, Nathalie 107

Land, the 4-32

Language 17, 34, 35, 41-43, 58, 61, 71, 75, 91, 92, 95, 99, 103, 173

Law 35, 65-67, 143

Layoffs 143, 145

Le droit civil 65, 66

Lee-Gartner, Kerrin 107

Legal system 65

Lieutenant governor 61, 63

Literacy 75

Literacy, computer 69

Literature 92

Lougheed, James 63

Lumber 13, 19, 139, 141, 149

MacDonald, John, A. 63

MacNeil, Rita 103

Macpherson, Duncan 15

Magazines 95, 97

Maillet, Antonine 57

Main Street Canada 91

Manitoba 11, 15, 17, 25, 41, 42, 51-53, 115, 127, 129, 149, 159

Manufacturing 21, 119, 134, 137, 139, 141, 142, 143, 147, 149, 151, 163, 165

Maritime Provinces 21, 137

Marriage 39

McLuhan, Marshall 67, 141

Meech Lake Accord 58

Menuhin, Yehudi 89

Mexico 15, 41, 142

Micmac Indians 19

Mineral production 163

Minerals 13, 17, 19, 63, 139, 163

Mitchell, Joni 103

Mitchell, W.O. 7, 33

Monarchy 58, 61

Montgomery, Lucy Maud 92

Moore, Mavor 85

Mowat, Farley 93

Multiculturalism 35

Murder rate 169-171

Murray, Anne 103

Museums 91

Music 71, 85, 89, 90, 92, 102, 103, 105

National Research Council 135

Natural regions 4-10

New Brunswick 10, 11, 19, 21, 27, 42, 43, 51, 149, 151

New Zealand 7, 147

Newfoundland 4, 9, 11, 13, 19, 21, 23, 27, 42, 43, 49, 65, 92, 147, 149, 151

North American Aerospace Defence Command 173

North American Free Trade Agreement 142

North Atlantic Treaty Organization 173

North magnetic pole 5

Northwest Territories 11, 13, 23, 34, 41, 42, 47, 63, 65, 67, 75, 134, 151

Norway 169

Nova Scotia 10, 11, 19, 21, 23, 25, 27, 42, 45, 49, 63, 134, 149

Nuclear power 141, 163, 165

Oil 11, 13, 17, 21, 141, 154, 165

Old Age Security 79

Olympics 107

One-parent families 34, 37, 39, 45, 47, 51

Ontario 9, 11, 17, 19, 25, 29, 35, 42, 43, 51, 63, 65, 69, 75, 85, 95, 99, 102, 107, 135, 143, 145, 149, 153, 165

Opera 85, 89, 90

Organization for Economic Cooperation and Development 75, 134, 143, 147, 154, 160, 161, 163, 165

Osler, William 73

Pacific Ocean 7, 25

Pacific Rim 141, 149

Paleoindians 10

Paleozoic era 9

Paper 19, 21, 141, 149

Parliament 58, 61, 63, 65, 66, 71, 169

Peacekeeping 160

Pension funds 78

Pension, disability 79

Performing arts 85, 87, 90, 91

Periodicals 95, 97

Petroleum and gas industry 137

Philippines 41

Place Royale 91

Pleistocene epoch 4

Population 34

Postsecondary education 75, 76

Potatoes 19, 21, 49, 151

Prairie Provinces 15, 25, 149

Prime Minister 61, 66

Prince Edward Island 10, 11, 21, 27, 41, 42, 49, 53, 92, 149, 151

Productivity 134, 143, 154

Provincial government 61, 65, 67, 70, 135, 155

Publishing 84, 92, 93, 95

Pulp 13, 19, 21, 141, 149, 151, 160, 163

Quebec 11, 17, 19, 25, 35, 42, 43, 51, 58, 63, 65, 66, 75, 95, 97, 99, 105, 137, 149, 153

Quebec Cinema Act 99

Radio 63, 70, 71, 101, 102, 103, 105

Rainforest 13, 119

Recession 73, 87, 90, 95, 97, 134, 137, 139, 142, 143, 145, 147, 151, 153

Religion 34, 43, 45

Remote sensing 141

Report of the Special Joint Committee on a Renewed Canada 58

Research and development 72, 76, 135

Retail stores 154

Robertson, Heather 91

Rocky Mountains 13, 17, 25

Royal Canadian Mounted Police 67

Royal Winnipeg Ballet 87

Ryga, George 84

Sarcee Indians 15

Saskatchewan 9, 11, 15, 17, 21, 41, 42, 53, 75, 92, 149

Schafer, R. Murray 89

Scientists and technicians 167

Secondary schools 75

Senate 59, 63, 65

Seniors 34, 39, 41, 51, 53, 78, 79

Service economy 151

Smoking 41, 77, 166

Social covenant 59, 76

Social programs 134

Social security 58, 63, 77, 78, 79

Society 58-82, 92

Sound recording 89, 103, 105

South Korea 141, 161

Spending 65, 135, 139, 153, 154, 155

Sport Canada 107

Spouses' Allowance 79

Statistics Canada 34, 37, 39, 69, 71, 75, 77, 78, 85, 87, 135

Statute law 65

Stock market 139

Suicide 45, 171

Supreme Court of Canada 66

Sweden 41, 166, 167, 169, 171

Swimming 77, 105, 107

Symphonies 89

Talon, Jean 91

Tax Court 66

Taxation revenue 135, 154

Taxes 35, 139, 153, 154, 155

Telecom Canada 70

Telecommunications 70, 72, 73, 134, 141, 163, 165

Telefilm Canada 99

Teleglobe Canada 70

Telephone 70, 72, 73, 165

Telesat Canada 70

Television 70, 71, 73, 101, 102, 105, 169

Theatre 85, 87, 102

Theatre du Nouveau Monde 85

Time zones 4

Tourbin, Dennis 110, 130

Tousignant, Serge 111, 117

Trade 63, 65, 78, 95, 135, 139-142, 149, 151, 160-166

Trade partners 135, 139-142, 161

Transportation industry 149

Unemployment 45, 49, 73, 95, 115, 134-139, 142-145, 149, 151, 153

Unemployment insurance 134, 135, 154, 155

Unemployment rate 135, 143, 145, 167

United Kingdom 41, 73, 141, 142, 143, 145, 160, 161, 166

United Nations 29, 73, 79, 160, 166-171

United States 4, 19, 29, 35, 41, 61, 73, 76, 79, 85, 95, 97, 99, 101, 102, 103, 141, 142, 143, 145, 149, 154, 160, 161, 163, 165, 166, 167, 169, 171, 173

Unitel 70

Universities 41, 72-76, 87, 151, 171

Veterans' benefits 135, 154, 155

Videocassette recorder 71

Visual art 90, 110-131

Voisine, Roch 103

Walking 77, 105, 107

West Coast 25, 53, 119, 149

West Coast tribes 13

Western Cordillera 4, 7

Wheat 9, 15, 17, 53, 139, 141, 149, 160, 166

Widowhood 37

Workforce 41, 134, 137

World Bank 134, 160, 173

Yemen 160

Yugoslavia 101

Yukon 7, 9, 11, 13-15, 23, 41, 42, 43, 47-49, 63, 65, 67, 151

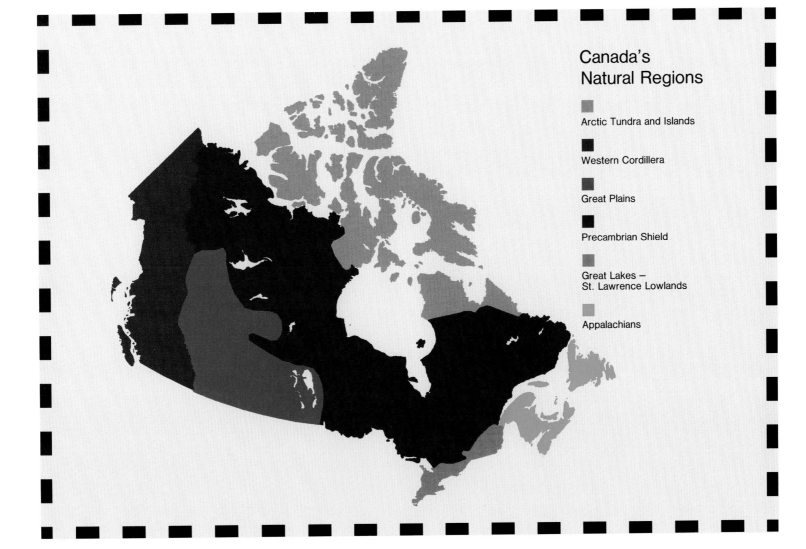

Canada's
Natural Regions

Arctic Tundra and Islands

Western Cordillera

Great Plains

Precambrian Shield

Great Lakes —
St. Lawrence Lowlands

Appalachians

Canada

Scale 1:20 000 000 or 1 centimetre represents 200 kilometres

CANADA – 1:20 000 000

POPULATED PLACES 1981
- ⊛ Federal Capital
- ⊛ Provincial Capital
- • Other Populated Places

BOUNDARIES
- –··–··– International
- –·–·– Provincial and Territorial
- ········ District
- ········ Unsurveyed
- – – – Dividing Line – Canada and Greenland

TRANSPORTATION
- ◆—◆ Trans-Canada Highway
- Principal Roads
- – – – Ferry
- Railway

All offshore islands in Hudson Bay, James Bay and Hudson Strait are part of the Northwest Territories.

Copies of this map may be obtained from the Canada Map Office, Energy, Mines and Resources Canada, Ottawa, or your nearest dealer. Quote MCR 132.

This map is based on information taken from map sheet number MCR 132 copyright 1987.

© Her Majesty the Queen in Right of Canada with permission of Energy, Mines and Resources Canada.